# FRIENDS OF THE COURT

# FRIENDS OF THE COURT

*The Privileging of Interest Group Litigants in Canada*

Ian Brodie

State University of New York Press

Published by
State University of New York Press, Albany

® 2002 State University of New York

All rights reserved

Printed in the United States of America

For information, address State University of New York Press,
90 State Street, Suite 700, Albany, NY 12207

Production by Kelli Williams
Marketing by Jennifer Giovanni

**Library of Congress Cataloging-in-Publication Data**

Brodie, Ian (Ian Ross)
 Friends of the court : the privileging of interest group litigants in Canada / Ian Brodie.
  p. cm. — (SUNY series in American constitutionalism)
 Includes bibliographical references and index.
 ISBN 0-7914-5299-9 (hc : alk. paper)—ISBN 0-7914-5300-6 (pbk. : alk. paper)
  1. Citizen suits (Civil procedure)—Canada. 2. Public interest law—Canada. I. Title II.
Series.

KE8404 .B76 2002
342.71'0854—dc21          2001049304

10 9 8 7 6 5 4 3 2 1

To my father and the loving memory
of my late mother

૨૦

# CONTENTS

# ACKNOWLEDGMENTS

The author gratefully acknowledges permission to reprint excerpts from the following publications:

George Radwanski. *Trudeau*. Toronto: Macmillan, 1978. Permission granted by George Rodwanski.

House of Commons, Committee on Human Rights and Status of Disabled Persons. *Court Challenges Program*, Issue #15. (December 1989); and House of Commons, Sub-Committee on Equality Rights. *Equality for All*, Issue #29 (October 1985). Permission granted by the House of Commons.

Richard C. Cortner. "Strategies and Tactics of Litigants in Constitutional Cases," *Journal of Public Law* 17 (1968): 287–307. Permission granted by the Emory Law Journal.

Kenneth P. Swan. "Intervention and Amicus Curiae Status in Charter Litigation." In *Charter Litigation*, ed. Robert J. Sharpe. Toronto: Butterworths, 1987.

Philip L. Bryden. "Public Interest Intervention in the Courts," *Canadian Bar Review* 66 (1987): 490–528. Permission granted by the author and the *Canadian Bar Review*.

Ian Brodie. "Lobbying the Supreme Court." in *Political Dispute and Judicial Review*, ed. Hugh Mellon and Martin Westmacott. Toronto: Nelson, 2000.

Rainer Knopff and F. L. Morton. *Charter Politics*. Toronto: Nelson, 1992.

Chapter 4 was first published as Ian Brodie, "The Market for Political Status," *Comparative Politics* 28 (1996) 253–271. Chapter 5 was first published as Ian Brodie, "Interest Group Litigation and the Embedded State," *Canadian Journal of Political Science* 34:357–376.

And lastly, the author would like to thank the Smallman Publication Fund of the UWO Faculty of Social Science for its support of this project.

# INTRODUCTION

Since the early 1980s, the Supreme Court of Canada has been a remarkably activist tribunal. In recent years, it has forced Alberta to extend its human rights code to protect against discrimination based on sexual orientation (*Vriend* 1998). It has required Canadian governments to extend spousal benefits to same sex couples (*MvH* 1999). And it has disrupted resource management policies by extending aboriginal rights (*Sparrow* 1990; *Marshall* 1999). During the course of its history, Canada has seen its courts make active use of the power of judicial review from time to time. But the Supreme Court's recent record of activism is unprecedented in scope. Moreover, despite having imposed policy losses on many governments and other political interests, the Court's activism has not yet sparked a notable political backlash. Some Canadian academics have criticized the Court for being too active, but even more have criticized the Court for not being active enough. Almost none of the academic criticism has filtered through to popular politics, and even the few muted criticisms that have been floated hardly compare with the kind of "court bashing" the U.S. Supreme Court provoked in the 1930s or the 1960s.

Even more remarkably, this activism has gone unchallenged during a time of nonstop attempts at high profile, comprehensive constitutional reform. In 1982, the Canadian government, under

Prime Minister Pierre Trudeau, succeeded in having the British Parliament insert the Canadian Charter of Rights and Freedoms in Canada's constitution, and then end the British role in future constitutional amendments. Since this "patriation" of the constitution, Canadian political leaders have tried three times to have massive packages of constitutional amendments ratified—the 1987 Meech Lake Accord, the 1990 package to make the Meech Lake Accord palatable to its opponents, and the 1992 Charlottetown Accord. Each successive round of efforts failed, and the first two each led Canadian leaders to try comprehensive constitutional amendment again by expanding the reform agenda. By the time the Charlottetown Accord was being worked out, such traditional constitutional issues as the reform of federal institutions, the federal-provincial division of powers, and the status of Quebec within Canada, were joined by new ones such as entitlements to health care and social programs, and self-government rights for aboriginal groups. The political interests that were being hurt by the Supreme Court's activism could have proposed limits to the Court's power during any of these rounds of constitutional reform, but few of them did so. The Meech Lake and Charlottetown Accords did respond to provincial complaints that the Supreme Court was too closely tied to the federal government to adjudicate federal-provincial disputes by proposing to let provincial governments have a say in the appointment of Supreme Court judges. Yet, these three packages of proposed constitutional amendments had no proposals to restrict the Court's powers or broaden Canada's centralized method of appointing Supreme Court judges beyond allowing provincial governments into the process. Any of the political interests that have been set back by the Court's decisions could have attacked the Court in order to leverage more wide-ranging judicial reform onto the political agenda. At the same time, there have been almost no demands for legislatures to use the Charter's "notwithstanding" clause to undo the Court's Charter decisions. This clause allows the Canadian Parliament or a provincial legislature to immunize particular pieces of legislation from judicial review under many sections of the Charter of Rights by simple majority vote. Even this mechanism has rarely been used to undo the effects of the Supreme Court's activist judicial review.

This quiet acceptance of the Court's activism is not due to any inherent deference to judicial authority in Canada's political culture. In the 1930s, Canada saw a backlash against judicial activism, just as the United States did. The Judicial Committee of the Privy Council (JCPC), which was then the final court of appeal for Canadian cases, repeatedly frustrated the efforts of Canadian governments to enact welfare legislation and economic regulations like those of the New Deal. The activism of the JCPC provoked a vigorous outcry of criticism in legal and political circles. The Judicial Committee was so discredited by this criticism that, in 1949, the Canadian government was able to replace the JCPC with the Supreme Court of Canada as the country's final court of appeal. The 1970s saw a less-public round of criticism of Supreme Court. At that time, some provincial governments and lawyers complained that the Court was leaning too much toward the federal government in its decisions on the federal-provincial division of powers. Consequently, provincial governments began demanding a role in the process of appointing Supreme Court judges. Canadian history has seen the exercise of judicial review spark political backlashes and successful efforts at judicial reform.

At the same time that the Supreme Court has been engaged in this activism, it has also attracted new attention from interest groups. It is hard to study the Supreme Court of Canada these days without studying the role of interest groups. Groups representing feminists, civil libertarians, language minorities, unions, business, and others regularly appear before the Court to argue legal issues of interest to their members. Journalists rely on comments by interest group leaders in their reporting on the Court's work. Interest groups even lobby behind the scenes over who will be appointed to the Court.[1] Today, the Supreme Court is just as much a forum for interest group activity as cabinet, the bureaucracy, the House of Commons, or the Senate.

Kent Roach argues that the "newness" of this attention from interest groups is overstated (1993). Political and community interests have been using the courts to influence public policy for decades. He notes that a century ago, Roman Catholics and French speakers in Manitoba sued the provincial government to protect their language and schooling rights. In the 1920s, Canadian feminists sued the federal government to make women eligible for appointment to the Canadian Senate. In the 1950s, Jehovah's Witnesses in Quebec appealed to the Supreme Court when that province's government tried to suppress their religious activities. For many decades, business interests have also used court action to roll back economic regulation (Mallory 1954). Roach is correct that various interests have often had recourse to the Canadian judicial process. However, the interest group litigation the Supreme Court has seen over the past twenty years is different. Until the 1970s, most interest group litigations were short-term, one-time affairs aimed at undoing a single set of government actions. Since the 1970s, the Supreme Court and other Canadian courts have seen a new kind of interest group activity—not sporadic efforts by loosely organized communities or ad hoc coalitions, but systematic, planned litigation campaigns by groups organized to wage long-term battles in the courts.

This book argues that these two phenomena—the Supreme Court's new round of judicial activism and the growth of litigation by interest groups—are linked. The Court's willingness to accept interest groups in its work has legitimized the Court's activism and, in turn, the Court's activism has legitimized its willingness to accept interest groups in its work. What makes this marriage of interests possible is the concept of the "disadvantaged group." The idea that because the other institutions of government cannot treat certain groups justly, the courts must step in and use their powers to vindicate the rights of these groups neatly legitimates activist judicial review if the courts work with politically disadvantaged groups. The concept of the disadvantaged group, which was first proposed in Justice Stone's famous footnote to the U.S. Supreme Court's decision in the *Carolene Products* (1937) case and was later adopted by political scientists in the political disadvantage theory of interest group litigation, in effect unites a court and a set of political interests under a common agenda.

The idea that a final court of appeal needs a social or political constituency to bolster its position in a political system is not novel. Hamilton underlined the relatively weak position of the U.S. Supreme Court in that country's system of government in *Federalist 78*. He noted the Court would need to rely on the cooperation of the other branches of government to have its decisions enforced. Mark Silverstein (1994) argues that the power of the U.S. federal judiciary, including the Supreme Court, depends on whether it is supported by important economic and political interests. In the 1890s, the U.S. Supreme Court's use of the judicial review power gained the support of mercantile capitalists. These allies rallied to the Court's side when it faced criticism for its work. In the 1930s, when the Court tried to use judicial review to hold back Roosevelt's New Deal, it found that laissez-faire interests could not defend the Court from political attacks. Roosevelt threatened to reconstitute the Court, and once new appointees took their seats on the bench, the Court retreated in its use of the judicial review power. It restricted the scope of the federal judicial power and allowed the other branches of government to build the contemporary American welfare and regulatory state. Later, as the New Deal coalition matured, the Court renewed its activism, but in the realm of civil rights rather than economic regulation. This gained the support of important constituencies in the New Deal coalition. Silverstein's analysis suggests that a powerful judiciary can only emerge when the judiciary has powerful interests backing it. When the Court is without effective allies, it risks dire consequences at the hands of politicians in the other branches of government. Knight and Epstein (1996) explain the emergence of judicial review as the product of strategic political choices by the U.S. Supreme Court in its defining years during the Jefferson administration. Courts may not self-consciously seek political allies in crafting their decisions, but state institutions, including courts, grow in political power as their activities coincide with the needs of politically powerful interests and lose political power when they lack such constituencies.

Charles Epp has recently written a major account of the growth in interest group litigation, what he calls the "rights revolution," in several countries, including Canada (1996). Canada, he notes, has enjoyed a "vibrant" rights revolution since 1960s (156). He attributes the growth of Canadian interest group litigation to several factors. First, Canadian political culture has become more conscious of rights issues since Trudeau proposed a constitutional bill of rights in the late 1960s. Secondly, a number of rights advocacy groups formed starting in the late 1960s—traditional civil liberties groups, followed by feminist, aboriginal, and disabled rights groups. These groups now sustain a network of activist lawyers interested in rights issues. Thirdly, the federal and provincial governments began funding criminal legal aid programs in the late 1960s and early 1970s. During the 1970s, the federal government started funding aboriginal and language rights litigation. Fourthly, the Canadian legal profession changed in important ways. It grew quickly in the 1970s, became more diverse and saw a number of large law firms established. Fifthly, the country's law schools became more independent from the bar, and more oriented toward legal criticism and activism. By 1982, Canadian law faculties had a large complement of young faculty that looked to the courts to take on a policy-making/law-reform role. Finally, Canadian governments established human rights commissions and law reform commissions to spur research and activism in rights issues. These agencies exchanged talent with the country's law schools, rights advocacy organizations, and other government departments. Epp attributes the growth in Canadian interest group litigation largely to non-state factors. Attributing the rights revolution to changes in Canada's political culture, its bar, and its legal academy emphasizes the social roots of interest group litigation.

Silverstein's analysis suggests there is another approach to the study of the Supreme Court and interest groups, one that would focus on how the Court positions itself relative to powerful interests in the exercise of activist judicial review. F. L. Morton and Rainer Knopff's Court Party thesis is an example of that approach (2000). Morton and Knopff cast a broader net than Epp. They attribute the activism of the Canadian courts to networks of activists and professionals they call the "Court Party." These networks bring together social reform-minded professionals and academics in public interest groups, government departments, independent government agencies, the criminal bar, and the law schools. Through their litigation, lobbying, research, publishing, and advocacy, they promote the typical "postmaterialist" agenda—"quality of life" issues, and social change in the name of equality. They look to the expansion of government and the entrenchment of redistributive programs so that government can remake society to be fairer based on gender, sexual orientation, race, and other kinds of identities. Morton and Knopff's central observation is that the Court Party is a political minority in Canada. Electoral politics is therefore not an advantageous arena for them. The Court Party prefers to advance its policy agendas through institutions that are insulated from electoral politics. The courts, quasi-judicial tribunals, and the administrative arms of government are arenas where the Court Party's professional skills and abilities can make up for their lack of electoral support. Morton and Knopff conclude that in the era of the Court Party, judicial review is not geared to restraining state power, but expanding it and directing it at wide-ranging social reform.

This book's analysis is complementary to the Court Party thesis. When the Supreme Court embarked on its new activism in the 1980s, it needed both a constituency and a justification to legitimate its new role in Canada's political order. Without a constituency of interests backing it and its program of action, the Court would have faced the same backlash that the Judicial Committee of the Privy Council faced in Canada, and that the American Supreme Court has often faced in the United States. The Court's solution, which it took from a loose coalition interest groups and sympathetic members of the legal academy, was to depict itself as the defender of disadvantaged groups. By importing the concept of disadvantaged groups into its jurisprudence, it gained those groups as allies. Whether this maneuver was deliberate or the inadvertent byproduct of the Court's decisions, the rhetoric of the disadvantaged group insulates the Court from criticisms of its activism. If the political process cannot protect the interests and rights of certain disadvantaged groups, then the courts must step in to correct the political process on behalf of the disadvantaged. Criticizing the courts would be criticizing the disadvantaged. Anyone who criticized the Court would be accused of wanting to attack disadvantaged groups.

Chapter 1 of this book traces the rise and fall of the concept of the disadvantaged group as a legal category, as a way of cementing the New Deal coalition, and as an analytical proposition in political science. It emerged from the suggestion in Stone's *Carolene Products* footnote that activist judicial review might be warranted where "discrete and insular minorities" are shut out of the political process. In the 1950s and 1960s, the U.S. Supreme Court picked up on this suggestion and began delivering important victories to racial and religious minorities, minorities that were important constituencies for the New Deal coalition. The concept of the disadvantaged group was then picked up in the development of the political disadvantage theory in American public law literature of the 1950s and 1960s. In Canada, the theory has become popular since the mid-1980s.

Chapter 2 looks at relations between the Supreme Court of Canada and interest groups empirically and historically. It focuses on the Court's treatment of interest group interveners. During the 1970s and 1980s, the Supreme Court struggled to find an appropriate place for interest groups in its work. It began to hear from a limited number of interest group interveners in the mid-1970s. Within a decade, this limited openness no longer satisfied the groups that wanted to participate in the Court's work. After the Charter of Rights was adopted in 1982, many groups expected the Court to play the kind of role the political disadvantage theory said it should play. Instead, the Court decided to clamp down on interest group intervention. Groups that were mobilizing for legal action reacted furiously, mobilizing the Court to change its approach. This chapter documents how, by the end of the 1980s, the Court had changed its treatment of interveners and now rarely refuses to hear from them.

Chapter 3 provides a complementary doctrinal treatment of the Supreme Court's changing approach to interest group intervention. As the Court took on an explicitly law-making role in the mid-1970s, it found it needed interest group interveners and began to hear from them in its appeals. Some writers have suggested that the Court clamped down on intervention in the mid-1980s because it wanted to clear the substantial backlog of cases it had built up. I suggest that the Court may have clamped down because of how it thought about its role in the early years of the Charter. In response to the Charter, the Court claimed to be the supreme interpreter of the Canadian Constitution, and provided a legalistic defense for that claim that denied the Court had a creative role in making the law. While legal commentators writing in law reviews and other legal publications praised the Court for its claims of judicial supremacy, they lambasted the Court for seeing its role in legalistic terms. In the early 1990s, the Court responded to these criticisms by adopting a more political approach to intervention, while at the same time maintaining a legalistic defense of the legitimacy of judicial review. This has led to tensions and contradictions in the Court's own view of its role in Canada's constitutional order.

Of all the Charter's provisions, the Section 15 equality rights guarantees provide the widest scope for interest group litigation. Under prodding by a coalition of interest groups, the Supreme Court has interpreted Section 15 as a remedial provision to help disadvantaged groups. Being recognized as "disadvantaged" now gives groups important benefits in Canadian constitutional law. Chapter 4 uses a rational choice modeling technique to demonstrate how the dynamics of status-seeking influence group choices about whether to engage in equality rights litigation. The model shows that status-seeking politics has intrinsic limits.

The concept of the disadvantaged group legitimizes judicial review because it assumes that groups emerge from civil society to oppose oppressive government actions. This view matches a wider perspective that judicial review of civil liberties is a battle between the state and private actors. Chapter 5 challenges the society-centered and pluralistic assumptions at work here. At the macro level, institutionalist approaches to political science have shown how the state shapes society and therefore shapes political demands. Middle-range work on interest groups has questioned pluralist assumptions about how interest groups are formed and persist. In Canada, state funding plays a major role in the formation and persistence of many kinds of interest groups, especially the kind that claims to be politically disadvantaged. Both macro-level and middle-range developments undermine the view of judicial review as a conflict between private and state actors. This chapter demonstrates that the Canadian government has encouraged groups to litigate in Canada, particularly through the Court Challenges Program. It therefore casts doubt on the concept of the disadvantaged group itself.

This book has its roots in a doctoral dissertation I prepared at the University of Calgary. My studies in Calgary were made possible by funding from the Social Sciences and Humanities Research Council of Canada (Doctoral Fellowship 752-94-1495), the Alberta Heritage Scholarship Fund, the Killam Trust, and the University of Calgary's Department of Political Science. Some of the data used here were collected with research grants from the

Department of Justice, the University of Calgary Research Grants Committee, and the University of Western Ontario. I thank all these institutions for their support.

I also thank the public officials I relied upon while conducting the research reported here. I thank the Honorable Mr. Justice John C. Major, the Honorable John Crosbie, and Avvy Go for generously allowing me to interview them. Their comments provided valuable insights throughout this book. The staff of the Court Records Office at the Supreme Court of Canada granted me access to their archives and patiently accommodated my research needs. Without their help, I could not have written chapter 2. The access to information staffs of the Departments of Canadian Heritage, Justice, and the Privy Council Office courteously processed my many requests for records.

Much of chapters 4 and 5 appeared in *Comparative Politics* and the *Canadian Journal of Political Science*. I thank the editors of these journals for permission to reprint them.

Several outstanding political scientists gave me wonderful guidance and comments. I particularly thank Rainer Knopff, Christopher Manfredi, Neil Nevitte, Don Abelson, Grant Brown, Sam Clark, Stan Drabek, Charles Epp, Thomas Flanagan, Roy Flemming, Roger Gibbins, Lori Hausegger, Butch Kamena, James Keeley, Miriam Lapp, Michael Lusztig, Leslie Pal, Anthony Perl, Fred Wall, Marty Westmacott, and Bob Young. Thanks to Marco Navarro-Genie, Dominique Navarro-Fournier, Mebs Kanji, and Chrissy Carberry for their help. Jane Walsh first convinced me how important interveners are. Judy Karwacki kindly provided me with her work on the Court Challenges Program. I also thank the reviewers for SUNY Press, *Comparative Politics*, and the *Canadian Journal of Political Science*. Remaining errors are mine, however.

Sonya Nerlund assisted me during my first trip to the Court's archives. Since I arrived at the University of Western Ontario, I have had the help of several talented research assistants. Thank you to Eunice Machado, Pamela Yu, Audrey Boctor, and especially Ryan Schmidt.

I owe the greatest debt to Ted Morton. Over the past decade, I have come to know him as a supervisor, advisor, collaborator, and friend. By balancing true scholarship, active citizenship, and a strong family life he set a good example for younger academics to emulate. Someday, he will get the chance to serve that term in the Canadian Senate that Alberta's voters gave him. Until then, I hope this is only one of many projects we can work on together.

Finally, I thank my dear wife, Vida. She endured the longest, crankiest hours at the end of the project.

# 1

# THE POLITICAL
# DISADVANTAGE THEORY

Much of the Canadian scholarship on the new judicial politics of the past twenty years depicts the courts and the Charter as havens for disadvantaged groups in society. Richard Sigurdson, for example, claims: "Not only has the Charter given women and other disadvantaged groups access to an additional arena of democratic participation, it has also signalled to those who resist progressive change that they cannot so easily ignore the claims of Charter rights-holders" (1993, 113). Gregory Hein enthuses about the prospect of the courts using their power to support groups that feel they lack political power, and "improve" democracy by protecting "disadvantaged minorities" (Hein 2000, 19). The heartiest praise is reserved for the Charter's equality rights provisions. According to Dean Lynn Smith, the equality rights have helped "less advantaged persons and groups in Canadian society" (1994, 60). While some scholars have questioned the capacity of the courts to produce social change, the view that the Charter and the courts are, or ought to be, havens for disadvantaged groups dominates the Supreme Court of Canada's Charter jurisprudence.

There are good reasons to imagine that this line of thinking is right. The courts are independent of the rest of the political process, and some Canadians have latched on to the idea that the judiciary is a forum where decisions are made for principled, rather than merely interested, reasons. Judges are protected from political accountability by the doctrine of judicial independence. They stand back from the political process. Since judges are free from the dirty business of political compromise and the need for reelection, they can inject more "principled" considerations into public life (Ely 1980). The Supreme Court of Canada has stated that, at least as far as the Charter's equality rights section is concerned, the courts will look more favorably on the claims of "discrete and insular minorities" (*Andrews* 1989, 599), or those suffering from "disadvantage, vulnerability, stereotyping, or prejudice" (*Law* 1999, 534). Judges, according to this line of thinking, stand up for the disadvantaged minorities that our majoritarian system of government inevitably marginalizes. Judicial politics is laudable because it gives justice to those who cannot get it elsewhere.

The theory that courts have, or should have, a special responsibility to protect disadvantaged groups emerged from the United States. In 1938, the U.S. Supreme Court first hinted at the possibility that some groups, some "discrete and insular minorities," were so marginalized in politics that the courts had a particular duty to uphold their rights. Later, in the 1950s and 1960s, the Warren Court picked up on this suggestion and began delivering important victories to racial and religious minorities. Encouraging the courts to deliver, or at least not blocking the courts from delivering, these victories kept constituencies in the Democratic Party's New Deal electoral coalition during those years. Political scientists then took up the idea that "politically disadvantaged groups" resort to litigation because they cannot get access to the rest of the political process. The "political disadvantage theory" of interest group litigation soon dominated American political science research on public law. Since the collapse of the New Deal coalition in the 1968 presidential election, however, the idea that courts should help politically disadvantaged groups is no longer as politically potent in the United States. At the same time, American political scientists have reconsidered the explanatory utility of the political disadvantage theory. Oddly, though, just as the political disadvantage theory lost its influence in American politics and scholarship, the concept of the disadvantaged group grew in importance north of the border. It has been taken up by academic writers in Canada and become the cornerstone of the Supreme Court of Canada's equality rights jurisprudence.

## THE EMERGENCE OF THE CONCEPT OF THE "DISADVANTAGED GROUP"

The concept of the "disadvantaged group" has its roots in the U.S. Supreme Court's retreat from judicial activism at the end of the 1930s. During the 1930s, the U.S. Supreme Court thwarted repeated efforts at national economic and social reform. When the Court struck down President Roosevelt's New Deal legislation, Roosevelt threatened to reconstruct the Court in order to ensure that a second attempt at the legislation would be upheld. Faced with this threat to its constitutional position, the Court's judges reconsidered their opposition to these reform efforts and backed down. Instead of continuing to thwart Roosevelt's efforts, the Court upheld the New Deal, and began to establish limits on the power of the federal courts to review economic and social legislation. The era of judicial self-restraint that followed allowed the president and Congress to stitch together a remarkable coalition behind the New Deal's promise of welfare legislation and economic regulation.

The Court was divided, though, on whether to extend judicial self-restraint to other areas of government activity. In his famous footnote to the 1938 *Carolene Products* decision, Justice Stone suggested that judicial activism might be warranted when legislation prevented "discrete and insular minorities" from participating in the political process. Fifteen years later, the judges of the Warren Court took Stone's suggestion as their duty. They elaborated a doctrine of "strict scrutiny" based on Stone's footnote (Powell 1982) and embarked on a new era of judicial activism in the service of racial, ethnic, and religious minorities. The highest point of the Warren Court's work was its effort to advance the black civil rights movement. There is no more famous example of the Court's efforts than the 1954 *Brown v. Board of Education* decision ordering the desegregation of American public schools. The groups that won in the Warren Court and their supporters were important constituencies in the New Deal coalition. The Court's activism of the 1950s and 1960s helped cement their support for the coalition. By the time of Kennedy's New Frontier and Johnson's Great Society programs, the Court's activism for these groups had the backing of the executive branch. "By linking the federal judiciary with Kennedy's New Frontier and Johnson's Great Society, the justices of the Warren Court were confident that judicial activism in the service of the disadvantaged would be embraced as the new definition of judicial liberalism" (Silverstein 1994, 49). Democrats had no reason to stop and every reason to encourage the Court to deliver victories to these "disadvantaged groups."

Many social scientists supported the Warren Court's new activism, and they followed the Court's lead by providing sympathetic analysis of the federal courts' work on behalf of disadvantaged groups. Arthur Bentley (1967 [1908]) and David Truman (1960 [1951]) had earlier broached the idea of the judiciary as an arena for group-based political competition. For both of them, litigation was series of battles between members of socially or politically active groups. Truman, for example, opened his discuss of interest groups and the judiciary with the bold declaration that "[t]he activities of the judicial officers of the United States are not exempt from the processes of group politics" (1960 [1951], 479). In the wake of Truman's work, American scholars produced influential case studies of interest group litigation. This literature emphasized that interest groups decided to go to court when they found little support for their causes in other political forums. Clement Vose studied interest group litigation to show how judicial review "constitutes an invitation for groups whose lobbying fails to defeat legislation to continue opposition by litigation" (1958, 25). His work on the NAACP's campaign against restrictive covenants argued that the organization saw litigation as its only choice for political action given that the U.S. Congress was hostile to its interests. "In the face of failures to gain concessions from Congress, due in large part to the power wielded by the Southern delegation . . . Negroes turned to the judiciary" (1955, 102). He later documented what he saw as the NAACP's carefully planned litigation on voting rights, housing, transportation, education, and jury service (1958, 23). By deliberate use of "strategic litigation," launching cases in hostile judicial districts to guarantee opportunities for appeal, groups such as the NAACP could advance their causes step by step through the courts. In the same vein, Jack Peltason (1955) argued that groups chose litigation when they could not win in other institutions. When the NAACP sought to become more aggressive in the 1930s, its leaders considered a variety of political strategies to combat segregation. Some of these strategies would have required cooperation from state legislatures and Congress, but NAACP leaders decided they could not win in the country's segregationist legislatures. Desegregation could win in the federal executive because black Americans were becoming an important constituency in presidential elections. The NAACP's leaders also saw potential in the judicial branch. The NAACP planned its lobbying and litigation campaigns accordingly (1955, 50). Moreover, this was not just a political strategy of "outsider" groups such as the NAACP. Peltason carefully noted that solidly establishment groups such as the laissez-faire interests of the late nineteenth century used it. When business gradually found that it could no longer win in state legislatures following the Civil War, business groups decided to overcome this political disadvantage by enlisting the Supreme Court as an ally with an ambitious, planned litigation strategy (53).

By the 1960s, once the Warren Court revolution was in full swing, studies of interest group litigation stated the academic political disadvantage theory more sharply. Richard Cortner (1968), in a seminal article on litigation tactics in constitutional cases, wrote that while many litigants are corporations and labor unions simply lobbying for the kinds of advantage in court that they also seek in the legislature, the executive, and the bureaucracy, other litigants

> are highly dependent upon the judicial process as a means of pursuing their policy interests, usually because they are temporarily, or even permanently, disadvantaged in terms of their abilities to attain successfully their goals in the electoral process, within the elected political institutions or in the bureaucracy. If they are to succeed at all in the pursuit of their goals, they are almost compelled to resort to litigation. (287)

He argued that the coalition supporting redistricting in *Baker v Carr* (1962) exemplified this kind of disadvantaged litigant. In this case, the winning litigants were unable to have state legislatures reapportion themselves. They were forced to go to court, and they prevailed there by using strategically planned campaigns of litigation. Similarly, Lucius Barker's article on third parties in litigation concluded, "[T]hose unable to achieve policy goals in other forums do not hesitate taking their cause to the judicial arena" (1967, 64). He referred extensively to *Brown* and the planned, strategic litigation that preceded it. He also referred to *Baker v Carr*. In both instances, he wrote, "Congress and the states, primarily responsible for fashioning such policy, refused to give relief to the aggrieved interest. The Supreme Court did" (42). Moreover, he explicitly endorsed this judicial action. "It might be," he wrote, "that there are some issues on which the judiciary must act as a safety valve for the elected political branches, providing leadership when it is reasonably ascertained that the elected institutions are either unwilling or unable to act" (64). *Brown* became such a storied case, it lent credibility to the political disadvantage theory.

By 1968, the political disadvantage theory was the preeminent explanation of interest group litigation in American social sciences. High profile litigation campaigns and courtroom victories in cases such as *Brown* certainly added zest to the idea that interests who were shut out of other political arenas could use planned, strategic litigation campaigns to gain political advantage in the courts. Inspired by the litigation of the NAACP, redistricting groups, the ACLU, and others, scholars happily noted how the American courts could make up for the majoritarianism of other political institutions by championing the causes of disadvantaged groups.

## THE DECLINE OF THE CONCEPT OF THE "DISADVANTAGED GROUP"

Just as the political disadvantage theory was gaining hegemony in academic circles, the importance of allowing judicial review to deliver political gains to disadvantaged groups began to decline in political circles. In the 1968 election the New Deal coalition, the keystone to Democrats' electoral success for a generation, collapsed. In part, the coalition collapsed because of the success of the courts in delivering political victories to some members of the coalition. The Warren Court's activism sparked a massive political reaction. In the South and elsewhere, other supporters of the New Deal became concerned with what they saw as liberal judges handing out special privileges to blacks, thwarting the battle against crime, and debasing American morality on issues such as contraception and obscenity. By 1968, racial issues and Vietnam were dividing Democrats. Union members, white southerners, and northerners from recent immigrant groups began leaving the New Deal coalition. Nixon showed that Republican candidates could win votes attacking judges for imposing liberal values on American politics. When the Supreme Court pushed forward to declare a constitutional right to abortion and restrict the death penalty, it fed the movement against judicial activism. For twenty of the next twenty-four years, Republicans controlled the White House and the power to nominate federal court judges.

The political disadvantage theory also faced a series of attacks in the social science literature. The first attack began with Marc Galanter's famous speculation about why the legal system might privilege the "haves" in society (1974–1975). Courts and judges, rather than giving a hand up to the disadvantaged, help those who already have social and political resources. Galanter argued that advantaged elements in society have more resources and are therefore either "repeat players" in the court system or can buy the services of repeat players. Since the "haves" are usually repeat players in the courts, they play the game with a longer time horizon and can often play for advantageous rules over the long haul rather than victory in a single case. They can bring greater resources to a particular case and then make better use of them over time. The disadvantaged, by contrast, usually have only isolated, one-time interactions with the legal system. They do not have the resources to hire experienced repeat players and, in any case, would not play the game for the long term even if they could. The "party capability" literature that arose from Galanter's work largely confirmed his speculations. In their test of this theory, Wheeler et al. (1987) discovered that the "haves," particularly governments, did come out ahead, although modestly, in state supreme courts between 1870 and 1970. Songer and Sheehan found that the parties they assumed to have relatively more resources did gain a marked advantage in three federal courts of appeal during 1986 (Songer and Sheehan 1992). These parties also gained an advantage at the U.S. Supreme Court from 1953 to 1988, although the changing ideological balance of the Court seemed to matter more than relative resources in determining case outcomes. The Songer and Sheehan studies excluded cases involving nonprofit groups, public interest groups, churches, clubs, and so forth, and also used indirect rather than direct measures of litigants' resources. Nonetheless, the party capability theory studies do question whether disadvantaged groups get a hand up from the courts.

Other studies used other approaches to the question of judicial capacity but arrived at similar answers. Horowitz (1977), for example, raised doubts about the courts' abilities to act as effective policy makers. Drawing on four case studies of judicial involvement in making social policy, Horowitz hypothesized that decision making by adjudication often produces perverse results in complex policy areas. In particular, judges may find it impossible to produce the changes they wish to see in areas where many players have mutually exclusive interests. The bipolar and retrospective nature of adjudication hampers the judiciary's ability to manage issues with many interested parties. Horowitz is skeptical that judges can ever truly achieve the public policy aims that they seek to impose on other government institutions.

Rosenberg raised even deeper doubts about the judiciary's ability to bring about wider social or political change. The "bounded nature of constitutional rights" means courts cannot handle "many significant social reform claims, and lessens the chances of popular mobilization" for reform (1991, 13). Most legal rights secure "negative" freedom and therefore cannot readily create positive political outcomes. The judicial process also usually forces advocates of social change to fragment their cause into many small cases. Moreover, the judiciary is not truly independent (15). Political actors control the appointment process, and in the United States, courts have seldom departed from the mainstream of public opinion. The U.S. Supreme Court in particular regularly defers to the position of the Solicitor General in litigation. Finally, Rosenberg reiterates Horowitz's concern that "courts lack the tools to readily develop appropriate policies and implement decisions ordering significant social reform" (21). Perhaps Rosenberg's most damaging attack on the political disadvantage theory is his appraisal of the black civil rights revolution of the 1950s and

1960s. He argues that the courts played only a small role in promoting the civil rights agenda. *Brown*, for example, did almost nothing to desegregate schools. The federal courts only began to play a role in desegregation after Congress passed its 1960s civil rights legislation. *Brown* did not even have an indirect effect on the desegregation campaign. The case did not increase the political saliency of civil rights issues. It had no measurable impact on press coverage, (111–116).[1] It did not figure in the legislative debates on civil rights of the 1950s or 1960s (118–121). White opinion on civil rights issues began to liberalize after World War II and *Brown* had no impact on this trend (121–128). Finally, the case did not figure in any mobilization efforts by civil rights leaders, even for the Montgomery bus boycott (131–134).[2] Instead, Rosenberg attributes the success of the civil rights movement to social and economic changes underway in the United States after 1945. Similarly, he argues that the abortion rights movement, the criminal rights movement, and the environmental movement also succeeded because of nonjudicial factors. Even the reapportionment of state legislatures, which began soon after *Baker v Carr*, failed to deliver the kind of social reform its proponents had hoped it would (293–303). Yet, Rosenberg does think the courts can sometimes help disadvantaged groups. They can help bring about social change if: the law provides a firm base for the desired changes, there is strong support for the change in Congress and the executive, public opinion does not vigorously oppose the change, and other policy actors are willing to go along (36).

The second line of attack on the political disadvantage theory began in the early 1980s. A new generation of students of interest group litigation started to go beyond single case studies to use quantitative methods to study interest group participation in the courts across the full range of policy issues. These studies show the narrow applicability of the political disadvantage theory. Some show that the number of "upperdog" groups outnumbers or equals the number of "underdog" groups in the U.S. courts (McIntosh and Parker 1988; Bradley and Gardner 1985). Others show that conservative groups are active in the court system, and their activities grew more quickly than those of "liberal" groups in the 1970s did. Still others show that civil rights cases are only a small part of the dockets of the U.S. federal courts. Civil rights litigation is only a small part of the universe of interest group litigation (McIntosh 1984). Moreover, interest groups are not any more successful than others in the U.S. federal district courts (Epstein and Rowland 1991) or the U.S. Supreme Court (Songer and Sheehan 1993).

Quantitative measures of political disadvantage, "underdogness," or liberality are fraught with problems of operationalization. Some researchers have used tangible organizational resources such as staff levels (Scheppele and Walker 1991) or budget (Bruer 1988) to measure disadvantage or underdogness.[3] None of these studies has attempted to measure the specialized legal or policy expertise that an organization might be able to mobilize to offset its lack of tangible resources. Furthermore, an unthinking equation of underdogs with liberals and the politically disadvantaged obscures the real differences between the categories (Olson 1990, 857). Bradley and Gardner (1985), for example, distinguish the upperdog-underdog categorization, which they use, from the liberal-conservative categorization that O'Connor and Epstein (1983) use. While their sociopolitical resources identify upperdogs and underdogs, liberals and conservatives are identified by their sociopolitical resources and their ideology.[4] "Politically disadvantaged" is a different category again. The political process can obviously give advantages to underdogs, upperdogs, ideological liberals, and ideological conservatives. Although is important to keep these different categories distinct, the verdict that emerges from this line of attack is that the political disadvantage theory described only part of the universe of interest group litigation.

Wasby (1984, 1995) and Tushnet (1987), for their part, have both questioned whether the most successful litigation campaigns over race were all that planned or strategic to begin with. Tushnet reconsiders the NAACP's litigation to end segregated education in the three decades leading up to *Brown*. He finds that divisions within the organization and uneven support from the broader black community meant its litigation strategies were always in flux and not the product of a master plan. Wasby looks at later race relations litigation by the NAACP and other groups. He concludes that these litigation campaigns were not carefully planned or strategic. Instead, the campaigns often responded to organizational and short-term imperatives. These studies question the idea that highly disciplined and centralized groups sponsor test cases across the country, wherever they might be of help to a cause.

By questioning the court's capacity to act as effective policy makers or social reformers, Galanter, Horowitz, and Rosenberg undermined the picture of the courts as safe havens for anyone, let alone politically disadvantaged minorities. Rosenberg's meticulous demonstration that court action had little independent impact on the social conditions of American blacks is particularly damaging. These were important new findings about the judicial capacity to bring about social change. Combined with the evidence that ethnic and religious minorities were not the only groups suing, and winning, in the U.S. courts, and that ethnic and religious minorities probably never were canny, strategic litigators in the first place, they led American scholars to reject the political disadvantage theory by the mid-1980s.

## THE CONCEPT OF THE DISADVANTAGED GROUP IN CANADA

Just as American academics were questioning the political disadvantage theory, Canadians began to find it persuasive. Today, many observers conclude that the courts are, or should be, havens for disadvantaged groups. Richard Sigurdson argues that the Charter is good for Canada, and improves Canadian democracy, because it has produced victories in the areas of due criminal process, abortion, voting, pay equity, welfare state benefits, and benefits for same sex couples. These are "victories for underprivileged individuals and groups" and they "enhance, rather than undermine, the democratic nature of our society" (1993, 108). The Charter "certainly does not guarantee that less advantaged groups will be given the means to overcome oppression and inequality," but it does recognize the "special needs of those who have historically been targets for discrimination" (109). It therefore helps prevent the worst rights abuses and symbolizes our commitment to respect others. Gregory Hein analyzes the litigation of groups he calls "judicial democrats"—aboriginal groups, civil libertarians, and New Left activists. These groups, he argues, have the greatest potential to influence public policy through litigation because they are motivated by the idea that litigation can enhance democracy. If the Canadian courts listen to groups that lack political power, they can "protect vulnerable minorities and guard fundamental freedoms" (2000, 5). Judicial democrats believe, according to Hein, that litigation can make Canadian institutions "more accessible, transparent and responsive" so long as the courts listen to "a diverse range of interests, guard fundamental social values and protect disadvantaged minorities" (19).

Some look particularly to the equality rights section in the Charter of Rights. This section reads:

> 15. (1) Every individual is equal before and under the law and has the right to the equal protection and equal benefit of the law without discrimination and, in particular, without discrimination based on race, national or ethnic origin, colour, religion, sex, age or mental or physical disability.
>
> (2) Subsection (1) does not preclude any law, program or activity that has as its object the amelioration of conditions of disadvantaged individuals or groups including those that are disadvantaged because of race, national or ethnic origin, colour, religion, sex, age or mental or physical disability.

Lynn Smith, a legal academic and volunteer for the Women's Legal Education and Action Fund, thinks the proper way to evaluate the impact of the Charter's equality rights is to ask whether "equality rights have done anything to remedy inequalities affecting members of the most disadvantaged groups in our society" (1994, 62). Section 15's purpose is to counterbalance "certain kinds of inequalities," namely, "disadvantage based on the kinds of personal or socially attributed characteristics listed in the section" (62). Overall, Smith sees the Charter's equality rights as achieving this purpose. Elizabeth Shilton, another LEAF activist, chips in that section 15 is "an instrument to promote equality for the disadvantaged" (1992, 658).

This is not to say that the main tenets of the political disadvantage theory have gone unchallenged in Canada. Various leftist scholars have mounted attacks on the Supreme Court's use of its new Charter powers, attacks that implicitly repudiate the theory. Mandel (1989) advances a neo-Marxist attack. He claims that judicial review has a profound class bias against the truly disadvantaged groups of capitalist society. Bogart (1994), following Rosenberg's analysis of the American Supreme Court, questions whether the Canadian courts can bring about social change. Litigation as a political tool is biased toward liberalism, in his account. Hutchinson (1995) advances a postmodern attack based on the idea that "rights talk" cannot adequately confront the reality of oppression and private economic power (see also Bakan 1997).

Indeed, there are few examples of courts providing aid to disadvantaged groups in Canadian history. Canada's courts had done little to help Canadian Indians, arguably the country's most discrete and insular minority. The Canadian government, like the American government, interned Japanese Canadians during World War II and Canadian courts, like American courts, failed to take remedial action. In the 1950s, the Supreme Court did eventually respond to the Duplessis government's persecution of the Jehovah's Witnesses with fits and starts of civil libertarian activism. Consequently, some partisans of the Witness cause wrote favorably about how judicial action could protect threatened minorities (Botting 1993; Kaplan 1989; Berger 1982). Yet, when Parliament adopted a legislative Bill of Rights that gave the courts the power to review federal legislation in 1960, it took the Supreme Court twenty-five years to respond with a significant activist decision using the bill.[5] Judges did not use the bill of Rights to reform Canada's criminal law. Canadian feminists found Canada's courts were unwilling to use the bill to reform Canada's abortion law (*Morgentaler* 1976), its laws governing Indian status for women who married non-Indian men (*Lavell and Bédard* 1974), and the pregnancy leave provisions of the Canadian unemployment insurance program (*Bliss* 1979) (Hosek 1983). As Peter McCormick (1993) shows, over the long run the "haves" have come out ahead in the Supreme Court of Canada.

Even when explicit constitutional guarantees were available to help disadvantaged Catholic and French-language minorities, the courts did not intervene on their behalf. In 1915, the Ontario government forbade the province's Catholic schools from using public funds for secondary schooling. Catholic

schools had enjoyed the right to public funding since Confederation and that right seemed clearly protected in the BNA Act
(Schmeiser 1964, 141). Yet, the Ontario courts, the Supreme Court
of Canada, and the Judicial Committee of the Privy Council all
refused to uphold Catholic school rights by overturning Ontario's
decision.[6] In 1890, the Manitoba legislature abolished French as
an official language of the province, and ended public funding of
Catholic schools. Both decisions almost certainly violated the
*Manitoba Act, 1870*. Yet, at the time only one county court judge
overturned the official language legislation, and his decisions were
ignored (Mandel 1989, 111–116). The Supreme Court did uphold the rights of Manitoba's Catholics to public funding for their
schools (*Barrett* 1891), but the Judicial Committee reversed that
decision on appeal the next year (*Barrett* 1892). The Manitoba
schools question became a national political issue that was eventually resolved by a political compromise (Wiseman 1992, 711–
712). In both Ontario and Manitoba, the Canadian courts failed
to protect politically disadvantaged minorities even when they had
relatively clear constitutional provisions on their side. The overall
treatment of politically disadvantaged minorities by the Canadian
courts hardly warranted any hope that the Charter would be a
tool for political reform.

Despite this history, the Supreme Court has incorporated the
concept of political disadvantage as the dominant mode of analysis
in its equality rights cases. In *Andrews v Law Society of British
Columbia*, the Supreme Court's first equality rights case, Justice
McIntyre repudiated the Supreme Court's Bill of Rights jurisprudence as a guide to interpreting the Charter's equality rights.
Instead, he decided that the purpose of section 15 is to stop
governments from burdening "discrete and insular" minorities
(1989, 599). Justice Wilson, concurring in McIntyre's analysis,
wrote that the purpose of section 15 was to protect those groups
"lacking in political power" and "vulnerable to having their interests overlooked" (1989, 152). These groups would be identified
not simply from the context of the laws being challenged, but by
"the context of the place of the group[s] in the entire social,
political and legal fabric of our society" (152). In the follow-up
case of *Turpin* (1989), Wilson expanded upon her earlier com-

ments. The purpose of section 15, according to her reasoning, is to remedy or prevent "discrimination against groups suffering social, political and legal disadvantage in our society." Such groups would be identified by "indicia of discrimination such as stereotyping, historical disadvantage or vulnerability to political and social prejudice" (1989, 1333). In more recent equality rights cases, the Court has gone on to say that historical disadvantage is not the only way to gain the benefit of section 15. The Court has also disavowed a strict division between advantaged and disadvantaged groups in its jurisprudence (*Miron* 1995; *Egan* 1995). Nonetheless, the Court has emphasized that "pre-existing disadvantage, vulnerability, stereotyping, or prejudice" are likely to be the "most compelling" factors in deciding section 15 claims (*Law* 1999, 534). Canadian scholars have noticed that this line of jurisprudence is inspired by American developments. In his textbook, Peter Hogg, Canada's foremost constitutional law scholar, notes, "The view that systemic disadvantage and political powerlessness are essential characteristics of the groups protected by s. 15 reflects a theory of equality that finds its origin in the famous footnote 4 of *United States v Carolene Products Co.* (1930)" (Hogg 1999, 1008). The political disadvantage theory, now discredited in the United States, has become the normative justification for Canada's constitutional equality rights jurisprudence.[7]

## CONCLUSION

The concept of the "disadvantaged group" has a long history, and a storied one in the United States. It emerges from the idea that activist judicial review is simply a way of correcting the failures of other political institutions in properly representing the full range of interests in society. It inspired the early political science work on interest group litigation in the United States. It has become a popular concept in Canadian academic work on the courts, and plays a central role in the Supreme Court of Canada's equality rights jurisprudence. Arguably, an important part of the concept's currency is the ready justification it provides for courts to make activist use of the judicial review power. There is a strong moral dimension the political disadvantage theory and the concept of the "disadvantaged group" brings some of the most shining moments of American jurisprudence to the fore.

How has this played out in Canada? Since the 1980s, there has been a dramatic increase in the role of interest groups in the judicial system. One indicator of this increase is the Supreme Court of Canada's willingness to accept interveners in its cases. The next two chapters document the Court's changing treatment of interest groups, particularly through the intervention mechanism. The Court's openness to interest groups is driven by the Court's rapid change of role in the 1970s and 1980s. During that time, the Court moved away from a focus on adjudicating individual, concrete, legal disputes. It took on a more explicit law-making role, and then embraced the invitation inherent in the Charter of Rights to embrace the supreme role in making constitutional law. Each of these stages in the Court's development has entailed changes in the way it treats interest groups. At the same time, as the Court has expanded its role in Canada's constitutional order, it has had to justify its expanded role. The moral stories embedded in the political disadvantage theory and the concept of the "disadvantaged group" have, I argue, helped immunize the Court from the kind of backlash final courts of appeal often face when they engage in activist use of the judicial review power.

# 2

## INTERVENERS AT THE SUPREME COURT OF CANADA

---

The Supreme Court of Canada sits atop the Canadian judicial system. It is by no means a typical Canadian court, but its decisions are the most prized resources the Canadian judiciary can bestow. Since the 1970s, it has become a particularly active law-making tribunal, and has had to grapple with the implications of its new role under the Charter of Rights. As the Court's role has changed, so has its relationship with interest groups. In the 1970s and 1980s, it struggled to find an appropriate place for interest groups, especially interest group interveners, in the judicial process. Under Bora Laskin's leadership in the 1970s, the Court began to accept more interest group participation in the judicial process. In the 1980s, as the groups involved in drafting the Charter of Rights began to mobilize campaigns of Charter litigation, they hoped the Court would be an ally of theirs. These groups were attracted to the Canadian Supreme Court by the U.S. Supreme Court's work on behalf of disadvantaged groups. The Canadian groups expected the Canadian Court to play the role the political disadvantage theory allotted it. The Court's activism in the early years of the Charter encouraged them in these beliefs. Yet, in the first few years after 1982, the Court actually clamped down on interest group participation in its cases. The groups that were mobilizing for litigation were outraged. They launched an unprecedented public campaign to convince the Court to change its approach. The Court responded to this profound challenge to its position and, by the end of the 1980s, embraced groups as full participants in its cases.

This chapter tells the history of how the Supreme Court has changed its treatment of interest groups. After a brief look at the principal ways in which interest groups can participate in court cases, it outlines the Canadian courts' approach to interest group litigation before 1970. It looks at the impact of the Trudeau reforms on the Court's role, and the Court's first steps toward changing the role of interest groups in its work. The analysis then turns to the mobilization of the 1980s, and the battle over the Court's approach to interest group intervention. This chapter's approach is quantitative and historical. Other issues raised by the Court's changing approach to interest group intervention are postponed until chapter 3. Here, the focus is on charting the Supreme Court's track record on handling interest groups, and the pressure that groups brought to bear to change it.

## Mechanisms for Interest Group Litigation

In common law legal systems, interest groups have two ways to participate in court cases. Whether a group wants to launch a one-time lawsuit over a specific government policy, or a strategic campaign that will influence the Court over several years, it can get its views into court in two ways. It can launch cases, either by sponsoring "test cases" or by filing suit in its own names. Alternatively, it can "intervene" in someone else's case and make its own arguments over the legal points at issue. To launch a lawsuit, a group must meet the "rules of standing" or find someone to sponsor who meets those rules. Until the late 1970s, Canada had quite restrictive rules of standing. It was difficult for interest groups to launch lawsuits over public policy. Groups could not sue a government, for example, just because they thought the government was acting unconstitutionally. Only individuals, corporations, or governments who had live, concrete legal disputes with other individuals, corporations, or governments could sue. Interest groups did not have much room to challenge legislation or government action on their own. They had to find someone who did have standing and then offer to pay their legal costs. Starting in 1975, the Supreme Court quickly rewrote the rules of standing, and by 1981, it had made it easier for interest groups to sue (*Thorson* 1975; *McNeil* 1976; *Borowski* 1981). Today, a group can launch a lawsuit over some aspect of the law if there is no other way for its constitutionality to be challenged in court.

Interest groups can also intervene in a case, and this is the more common route for Canadian groups to be heard before the Supreme Court of Canada. The common law courts have long depended on interveners, or amici curiae, to help them decide cases.[1] Lawyers once acted informally while waiting for their own cases to be heard by bringing legal points to the attention of judges. In a legal system built upon precedent, accurate reporting of decisions is a central cog in the machinery of justice. Until recently, a judge "had little more than his memory to serve him [in recalling past decisions], and thus there was great opportunity for error. Lawyers, awaiting hearing of their own cases, would speak out to assist the judge in his recollection . . ." (Levy 1972, 94). Amici also acted as interested advocates to represent people who were not represented in a case, to avoid injustices, and later to allow someone to speak for the public interest (Muldoon 1989, 113). The amicus procedure was available wherever strict adherence to the adversarial trial format would lead to an injustice. For example, as early as 1736 a judge who was faced with a case that could deprive a third party of his rights needed a way to hear from the third party. He allowed the third party to intervene as an amicus curiae. Although the rules of standing left little room for interest groups to litigate, the common law courts did not precisely define the amicus mechanism. It developed into "a highly adaptable instrument for dealing with many of the problems that arise in adversary proceedings" (Muldoon 1989, 696) and provided an opening for interest groups to participate in judicial proceedings.

A few Canadian interest groups appeared as interveners in reference cases during the early years of the twentieth century.[2] The Canadian Jewish Congress was probably the first interest group to intervene in a live case. In 1945, the congress successfully challenged the validity of a racially restricted covenant in the Ontario High Court in *re: Drummond Wren*.[3] However, *re: Wren* did not

mark the beginning of a great rush of interest groups into the
Canadian courts. More than two decades later, the Supreme Court
allowed the Lord's Day Alliance of Canada to intervene in the
1963 case *Robertson and Rosetanni*.[4] This was the Court's first Bill
of Rights case. The Lord's Day Alliance apparently wanted to
intervene because it feared that the Quebec Attorney General
"was not vigorously seeking to uphold" the federal Lord's Day
Act against a freedom of religion challenge (Friedland 1984, 98).

## AMICI CURIAE IN THE UNITED STATES

Interest groups began using the amicus curiae mechanism earlier in
the United States than in Canada. A handful of amici appeared before
the U.S. Supreme Court in the early years of the twentieth century.
In the 1950s and 1960s, the same groups whose work gave rise to
the political disadvantage theory were starting to appear before the
Court regularly. This amicus curiae activity attracted attention from
legal and political scholars in the United States.[5] The American experience with amici was studied by Canadians and referred to extensively by Canadian interest groups who wanted the Canadian Supreme
Court to accept more interest group interveners in the 1980s.

While American government officials appeared before the U.S.
Supreme Court as amici in the first half of the nineteenth century,[6]
private groups also used the mechanism in the early years of this
century. The Chinese Charitable and Benevolent Association of
New York first appeared before the Court in the 1904 *Ah How*
case. The NAACP first appeared before the Supreme Court in
1915, soon after it was founded, in *Guinn v U.S.*[7] Industries and
business associations began to appear in regulatory cases. Then the
ACLU and American Jewish Congress also began appearing before the Supreme Court (Barker 1967, 1018; Krislov 1963, 705–
708). By the 1930s, a few private groups were appearing "openly
as advocates on behalf of some group or class struggle desiring to
support the contentions of a party to the litigation" in a handful
of cases (Barker 1967, 1018).

The number of *amici* soon began to grow. In his landmark
analysis of amici curiae in the U.S. Supreme Court, Puro (1971)
looks at three eras of the Court's history: the Taft Court (1920–

1936), the New Deal Court (1937–1952), and the Warren Court (1953–1966). Amici participated in 10.5 percent of the Taft Court's cases, 20.3 percent of the New Deal Court's cases, and 31.4 percent of the Warren Court's cases (Puro 1971, 56), a remarkable growth over five decades. Excluding the uncharacteristic 1953–1956 period of low amicus activity, the later Warren Court (1957–1966) attracted at least one amicus in 35 percent of its cases (55). One follow-up study finds that amici participated in 53.4 percent of the Burger Court's cases between 1970 and 1980 (O'Connor and Epstein 1981–1982, 316).[8] Amici have appeared in more than three-quarters of U.S. Supreme Court cases since 1986 (Epstein, Segal, Spaeth, and Walker 1996, 647). One study concludes, "amicus curiae participation by private groups is now the norm rather than the exception" (O'Connor and Epstein 1981–1982,18). Other studies report broadly similar findings in the U.S. federal district courts and federal courts of appeal (McIntosh 1984, 1988).

What was driving this growth in amicus activity? Puro suggests that the amici curiae activity by "social defence organizations" was growing most quickly. These organizations appeared in only 1.2 percent of the Taft Court's cases, but in 14.4 percent of the New Deal and Warren Court's work (Puro 1971, 61). The ACLU, the American Jewish Congress, the National Association for the Advancement of Colored People, the Japanese American Citizens' League, and the American Jewish Committee were the busiest social defense organizations in the U.S. Supreme Court during these periods (Puro 1971, 64–65). These were the same groups whose litigation inspired the political disadvantage theory. Labor (1.1 percent, 8.3 percent, and 7.9 percent) and professional (2.2 percent, 6.1 percent, and 9.6 percent) organizations increased their amicus activity during these periods, but at less dramatic rates (Puro 1971, 61). Moreover, the growth in amicus activity took place in the newer areas of public law. According to O'Connor and Epstein, union law, sex discrimination, race discrimination, free press claims, and the freedom of information law were the kinds of issues most likely to attract amici between 1970 and 1980 (1981–1982, 316). The biggest jump in amicus participation between the 1928–1966 and 1970–1980 periods occurred in labor law, free press claims, race discrimination, and church-state relations cases (1981–1982, 317).

Although these numbers show impressive growth, they do not do justice to the long-term impact of amici in the academic literature. Politically disadvantaged groups were high profile users of the amicus mechanism, and academic writers devoted more attention to them than their numbers warranted in the 1950s and 1960s. Almost all these academic writers linked the amicus to the political disadvantage theory. Vose, for example, noted the importance of friendly amici in the NAACP's campaign against restrictive covenants (1955, 133–138). Later, he wrote that "[t]he frequent entrance of organizations into Supreme Court cases by means of the amicus curiae device has often given litigation the distinct flavour of group combat" (1958, 27). Lucius Barker remarked on the "particularly dramatic" growth in the filing of amici briefs, and argued that they were important in the leading desegregation and reapportionment cases (1967, 42). Samuel Krislov also published a long article tracing the evolution of the amicus mechanism (1963). Only Nathan Hakman (1966) dissented from the view that the amicus mechanism was an important tool for progressive, liberalizing public interest law. He found few instances of amicus participation in the Supreme Court's noncommercial cases from 1928 to 1968, and even less evidence of interest groups using systematic litigation strategies to achieve their objectives. On the whole, though, the near consensus of these commentators was that amici were critical participants in the Warren Court's greatest moral victories on behalf of disadvantaged groups. Beginning with the school desegregation campaigns and continuing through to the rewriting of U.S. criminal law in the 1960's, amici figured prominently in two decades of "social justice" victories in the Court.

## THE SUPREME COURT OF CANADA AND INTEREST GROUPS IN THE 1970s

The high profile of these cases, particularly the school desegregation cases, gave the literature on interest group litigation and amici curiae a certain profile in Canada. Observers started to think that a similar use of systematic litigation and amicus curiae intervention could improve the lot of Canadian groups that they thought of as politically disadvantaged. Six years before the Charter, Bernard Dickens pointed to the American use of the amicus as a model the Canadian Supreme Court should follow. "In the United States," he wrote, "the amicus curiae has come to enjoy a distinguished twentieth-century history in the promotion of minority interests . . ." (Dickens 1977, 672). He listed the ACLU, NAACP, and the American Jewish Congress among the "interest-groups presently active in the courts in defence of minorities" (672). One factor driving the development of the amicus curiae in the United States was

> the militancy of groups of activists of an almost unlimited range, but increasingly composed of socially committed, civil libertarian people, undertaking for the under-privileged and deprived what the better-educated articulate middle-classes did for themselves in movements for consumer and investor protection. (673)

Dickens noted that similar groups such as the CCLA, women's organizations, ethnic community groups, and Indian rights groups, were emerging in Canada.

Shortly before the entrenchment of the Charter, James West published a wide-ranging manifesto for invigorating the Canadian judiciary with American-style political activism (1979). He complained that the "judiciary's mandate to write law in bold letters remains as uncertain in the 1970's as it was when the Supreme Court became our final appellate tribunal in 1949" (West 1979, 1–2). Since he thought the amicus curiae had "served to politicize the American judicial process," he concluded that the Canadian court system could be politicized by opening it up to interventions by Canadian disadvantaged groups. Groups such as the NAACP and the ACLU had attained national prominence in the United States through "their efforts to enhance and protect minority interests in the legal arena" (1979, 1). He identified procedural, constitutional, and attitudinal barriers to making the judiciary an ally of the politically disadvantaged in Canada. A strong judiciary would achieve justice, and interest group amici would advise judges on what justice entailed. While West's view of the issue is simplistic, it is nonetheless a telling example of what lessons Canadian commentators were taking from the U.S. experience.

Interest in a more American approach to intervention arose just as the Supreme Court's place in Canada's constitutional order was beginning to change. Until the 1970s, the Court had a low political profile among Canadian political institutions. It did not become Canada's final court of appeal until 1949, and even after the abolition of appeals to the judicial committee of the Privy Council, the Supreme Court's judges saw their role as settling individual disputes rather than tackling public policy issues. Moreover addition, the Court did not control its own docket. Until 1975, a case could be appealed to the Supreme Court automatically if more than $10,000 was at stake. This rule meant that the Court spent much of its time deciding routine commercial lawsuits. Few of these cases raised new legal issues, but they took up the time and energy of the Supreme Court's judges all the same.

When Pierre Trudeau entered federal politics in the mid-1960s he intended to give the Canadian courts—including the Supreme Court—a bigger role as policy makers. Two factors motivated his efforts at judicial reform. First, he wanted to promote liberal law reform in Canada. As Minister of Justice, he had proposed legislation to loosen Canada's laws on abortion and homosexuality. He hoped that if the courts became more explicitly involved in policy making, they would advance the cause of law reform. Trudeau also hoped that increased judicial policy making would help to combat the disintegrative pressures in Canadian politics. He thought that expanded bilingualism in the federal government and improved access to French-language schooling outside Quebec would counter the appeal of nationalism inside Quebec. Even before he went into politics, he was well aware that bilingualism and expanded French-language schooling would not be universally popular across Canada. "It would not be realistic to rely upon good will or purely political action," to achieve these aims (Trudeau 1968, 48). The best way to implement his national unity solution was to amend the constitution to guarantee language "rights." This would convert issues of provincial language policy into questions of constitutional rights. The courts could then force the provinces to adopt greater bilingualism in their policies. Trudeau's planned Charter of Rights, which was to include fundamental freedoms and civil liberties as well as language rights, would also moderate the pressures of "centrifugal territorialism" that he thought threatened Canada's unity (Knopff and Morton 1985, 133). A Charter of Rights would give Canadians a sense of national citizenship that transcended provincial boundaries (Russell 1983; Knopff and Morton 1985; Mandel 1989).

To fulfill Trudeau's hopes, the Supreme Court had to be retooled. Trudeau implemented two reforms that shifted the Supreme Court's role away from adjudication and made it more of a policy maker. First, he began to appoint a new kind of judge to the bench, judges who were amenable to taking on a policy-making role. He appointed judges with experience in law reform and the academic world. Bora Laskin, who had been dean of law at the University of Toronto and a well-known critic of the Supreme Court's reluctance to get involved in policy making, went to the Court in 1970 and became chief justice in 1973. Two other former law deans (Beetz, LeDain), and a former member of the Law Reform Commission of Canada (Lamer) followed him to the Court during Trudeau's years as prime minister. These new judges wanted the Court to take an active role in making policy. By the mid-1980s, the Court was dominated by reform-minded judges eager to get involved in complex policy issues. Secondly, Trudeau gave the Court greater control over the cases it heard. By the early 1970s, many lawyers and politicians thought the Court should have greater control over its own docket. In 1974, Parliament agreed to abolish the right of appeal in cases involving more than $10,000. Only certain kinds of criminal cases and reference cases would still be able to be appealed by right.[9] Freed from hearing routine commercial cases, the Court could devote its time to cases with broader policy implications.

The Supreme Court's new judges readily accepted the challenge of their new role. They responded to Trudeau's program of judicial reform by changing the Supreme Court's pattern of work. They began by quickly transforming the Court's docket. The Court's work began to focus on higher-profile public law issues of national significance. According to Ian Bushnell's research (1982), in 1970–1971 the Court heard 151 cases, 83 percent of which arrived by right. Ten years later, the Court heard 117 cases, almost 74 percent of which arrived by leave of the Court. The Court

shifted its focus away from commercial disputes and toward con-
troversies in public law. Before 1974, the Court's caseload was
largely taken up with commercial appeals, but by 1983, public law
cases comprised 76 percent of the cases before the Court. In 1984
and 1985, the corresponding figures were 89 percent and 84
percent (Russell 1987, 347). They also abandoned the Court's
strict adherence to stare decisis, began sitting as a nine-judge bench
more often, and wrote fewer seriatim decisions, and started to
hear nontraditional types of evidence. Taken together, these changes
transformed the Court into an important political institution with
a significant role in developing Canada's public law and serving
the nation-building purpose of the Charter (Knopff and Morton
1985, 158–165).

The judges also changed their treatment of interest groups.
There were changes both in the approach to interest group intervention and Canada's law of standing. Bora Laskin led the Court
on the issue of interest group intervention. In 1973, before he
was appointed chief justice, the Court allowed women's and Indian groups to intervene in the *Lavell* (1974) case. This Bill of
Rights case challenged the policy of stripping Indian status from
Indian women who married non-status Indian men. Allowing
several interested parties to become involved in the case sent a
signal to the legal community. *Lavell* "gave the seal of judicial
approval to the admission of private non-parties before the highest
court to argue civil cases" (Dickens 1977, 674). Two years later,
as chief justice of the Court, Laskin solidified the *Lavell* precedent
by allowing several groups to intervene in the first *Morgentaler*
case, a challenge to Canada's abortion law (1976). The importance of these signals was not missed at the time. Dickens called
Laskin's decision to hear the interveners "almost as significant" as
the outcome of the case. *Lavell* and *Morgentaler* together, he
wrote, "pointed the way to the emergence of an authentic North
American procedural jurisprudence uniting Canada and the United
States of America" (Dickens 1977, 666). The Canadian Bar Association declared the two cases to be the "first significant change in
the Supreme Court of Canada's" treatment of interest groups
(CBA 1991, 22). The Supreme Court did begin to move towards
a U.S.-style intervener mechanism, but slowly. In the wake of
*Lavell* and *Morgentaler* groups did intervene from time to time.

The Court heard from thirty-five nongovernment interveners between 1976 and 1982, but also turned away sixteen others.

Soon after *Lavell* the Court began changing the Canadian law of standing. Up to that point, Canada had adhered to traditional rules of standing on public interest issues. The leading precedent had declared that no one had standing to challenge the constitutionality of legislation unless he or she was "exceptionally prejudiced" by it (*Smith* 1924, 331). Therefore, it was almost impossible for any private person or group to launch a public interest lawsuit. The Supreme Court began to change the rules in the 1975 case of *Thorson*. Thorson, a retired judge, went to court to challenge the Trudeau government's bilingualism legislation. The lower courts had all agreed that Thorson had no standing to challenge the law. But Laskin and a majority of the Court granted him standing on appeal. Although three of his colleagues dissented in the case, complaining that the Court was taking on a role it had no business assuming, Laskin declared that citizens had a right to "constitutional behaviour" from Parliament. Only the courts could ensure that Parliament would act constitutionally, and the rules of standing would have to change to allow the courts to decide on the constitutionality of legislation where no one could establish a traditional claim to standing (*Thorson* 1975, 138). A year later, in *McNeil* (1976), Laskin and the Court allowed a journalist to challenge Nova Scotia's film censorship laws even though theatre owners were directly affected by the legislation and could have met the existing rules of standing. Finally, in *Borowski* (1981), a majority of the Court let a male activist acting on behalf of the pro-life movement challenge Canada's abortion law. He claimed that the law did not provide adequate protection to the unborn. They ruled that any citizen could launch a constitutional challenge against legislation if there was no other way the constitutionality of that legislation could be raised in court. This "standing trilogy" of cases gave Canada one of the common law world's most lax laws of standing. Together, the three cases gave interest groups a wide range of possible test cases to sponsor or launch themselves.

Laskin has been lionized for his work in broadening the Court's approach to interest groups, but he became less enthusiastic about intervention and standing later in his career. For example, he was hesitant to allow too many interveners in the Court's cases. In

1983, the Court's registrar approached Laskin about allowing the noted judicial administration expert Carl Baar to intervene in the judicial independence case of *Valente*. Laskin fired back a curt memorandum declaring that "I am not going to let this kind of thing [intervention] get out of hand. The answer is plainly 'no.' "[10] Similarly, although he supported the Court's expansion of the law of standing in *Thorson* and *McNeil*, he dissented from the Court's decision to broaden the law even further in *Borowski*. His dissent sounded very "un-Laskin-like" (Morton 1992, 101), warning his colleagues about going too far in opening the Court's doors to political issues. If the Court granted Borowski standing, it would have to grant intervener status to groups on the other side of the abortion issue and allow them to wage their political battles in the judicial arena. This is the same Laskin who had welcomed the participation of abortion groups in the *Morgentaler* appeal in 1975. By 1981, he was beginning to see limits to the role of interest groups in the Court's work.

The Court's position in the Canadian constitutional order began to change during the 1970s. Activist judges with an interest in law reform increasingly staffed the Court. They had control over their own docket. The Court began to accept interest groups as interveners in its cases. The Court also loosened the country's law of standing and ensured a steady flow of constitutional challenges through the courts. As interest groups mobilized to influence the drafting of the Charter of Rights and planned litigation to follow up on their victories in that battle, they would push the Court to go even farther.

## MOBILIZING FOR LITIGATION

In 1980, the Quebec government held a referendum on declaring a form of independence for that province. In his campaign to defeat the referendum question, Trudeau promised that a "no" vote would lead to national constitutional reform. When the "sovereignty association" referendum question was defeated, the Trudeau government proposed a large package of constitutional amendments that would add a Charter of Rights to the Canadian constitution and then "patriate" the constitution from the British

Parliament. A number of interest groups became involved in the process of patriating the constitution and drafting the Charter. Once the Trudeau government decided to proceed with patriation unilaterally, without provincial support, and to strike a special joint committee of Parliament to canvass public input on constitutional reform, these groups had an institutional forum where they could advance their demands for changes to the government's reform package. They saw the Charter of Rights as an opportunity to pursue their interests in the courts and lobbied for wording that would favor their causes. Once they had secured favorable wording, they began planning to follow with litigation campaigns. To use Manfredi's terminology, they realized that they needed to convince the courts to promulgate favorable second order interpretive rules to give force to their victories over the first order rules in the Charter.[11] Feminists, in particular, drew lessons from the U.S. experience and decided to bring strategic litigation to Canada. They and the Canadian Civil Liberties Association (CCLA) both eventually settled on intervention as a component of their litigation strategies.

Canada's feminists energetically promoted a comprehensive Charter of Rights during 1980 and 1981 and were actively involved in drafting the document.[12] Canadian feminists had not been widely interested in legal approaches to equality before 1980, but when the first ministers tentatively agreed to devolve jurisdiction over divorce to the provinces in February 1979 (an agreement that never succeeded), many feminists began to mobilize around constitutional issues (Hošek 1983, 280–282). They fought bitter battles over the wording of the Charter of Rights throughout the patriation process, and even fought to have a government-sponsored conference on constitutional reform in February 1981. The result of these battles was "a strong constitutional guarantee of equality" in the new Charter of Rights (Razack 1991, 28–34). Feminists succeeded in having the nondiscrimination rights in the Charter renamed equality rights. More importantly, they had their version of section 15 incorporated "verbatim" into the government's draft (Knopff and Morton 1985, 153). Their version was intended to overturn the Supreme Court's interpretation of equivalent provisions of the Bill of Rights. In the end, they also had sexual equality rights exempted from the operation of the Charter's "notwithstanding clause," section 33. This was an impressive string of victories.

Since they had been directly involved in the battles over the Charter's drafting, Canadian feminists were well placed to pioneer the use of U.S. legal strategies, including the amicus curiae mechanism, in Canada (Manfredi 2000). When the Ad Hoc Committee of Women on the Constitution held its February 1981 conference on constitutional reform, the participants referred to the NAACP as a model for a women's law fund in Canada (Razack 1991, 36–38). The Canadian Advisory Council on the Status of Women, a government-funded agency, then commissioned three leading Canadian feminist lawyers to study the prospects for a women's law fund in Canada. Their 1984 report, *Women and Legal Action* (Atcheson, Eberts, and Symes 1984), argued that the time had come for such a fund. Its longest and most comprehensive chapter investigated the experience of every active U.S. legal defense group.[13] This chapter began by recounting the story of *Brown v Board of Education* (Atcheson, Eberts, and Symes 1984, 103). Thus, the leading example of the political disadvantage theory in action became a central justification for a feminist legal action organization in Canada. "The *Brown* case," the Report stated, "is a perfect example of how crucial and how effective public interest law can be" (Atcheson, Eberts, and Symes 1984, 104). The chapter then surveyed the U.S. literature on public interest litigation,[14] relying heavily on O'Connor's *Women's Organizations' Use of the Courts* (1980). The authors recommended the creation of a women's legal action fund in Canada, which would take "the systematic approach to litigation developed in the United States" (Atcheson, Eberts, and Symes 1984, 166), including participating as an intervener before the Supreme Court where this was possible.[15] In the wake of Brodsky and Day's finding (1989) that antifeminist interests were pursuing equality rights cases actively, intervention became a more important part of the eventual litigation strategy. A self-described "Toronto core" of women on the Ad Hoc Committee had been meeting under a number of names to organize a variety of Charter-related projects. In the summer of 1984, the authors of the CACSW report and a small group from the Toronto core began planning a legal defense fund (Razack 1991, 38–47). In April 1985, when the Charter's equality rights provision came into force, LEAF, the Women's Legal Education and Action Fund, was founded. As documented below, it has become the Supreme Court's top interest group intervener.

The Canadian Civil Liberties Association was also involved in the debates over the wording of the Charter's "reasonable limits," legal rights, and remedies sections. When the government released the January 1981 version of the Charter, it became apparent that the CCLA had won a stronger version of the "reasonable limits" section,[16] a host of expanded legal rights, and an explicit authorization of judicial remedies for Charter violations. The CCLA also eventually won a partial victory over the Charter's exclusionary rule (Knopff and Morton 1985, 153). Once the Charter was in place, the CCLA also intended to follow the example set by its American counterpart, the American Civil Liberties Union, and enlist the judiciary as an ally in its battles for such politically disadvantaged groups as accused persons and prisoners. The CCLA repeatedly urged the Supreme Court of Canada to open its doors to interveners. CCLA vice-president Kenneth Swan argued in 1986 that the "best example of the real value of public interest intervenors is found in the most sophisticated system of constitutional adjudication in the world, that of the United States" (1987, 39). He then listed a complete inventory of ACLU Supreme Court victories—*Miranda v Arizona* (1966), *Mapp v Ohio* (1961), *Furman v Georgia* (1972), *Poe v Ullman* (1961), and *Griswold v Connecticut* (1965)—all victories won as an amicus curiae. "The American experience," he concluded, "is the clearest possible indication" that "public interest intervention is a vital part of a mature constitutional adjudication system . . ." (41). "The welcome extended to intervenors by the United States Supreme Court is a welcome which our Supreme Court should emulate" (41). CCLA leaders were evidently well versed on the ACLU's success as an amicus.

By the time the first Charter cases were beginning to arrive at the Supreme Court, then, both Canadian feminists and the CCLA were planning to pursue systematic campaigns of litigation. Having won victories over the wording of the Charter in the constitutional amendment process, they needed to follow up by winning favorable interpretive rules in the judicial process. Citing the American experience, especially American cases made famous by the political disadvantage theory, they formulated American-style strategies for public interest litigation, including interventions in the Supreme Court. By 1982, the Supreme Court's place in the Canadian constitutional order had already begun to change, and there were good reasons to imagine that the Court would open its doors to interest group interveners.

## THE FIGHT OVER INTERVENTION

During the first five years of the Charter era, the Supreme Court proved to be ambivalent about its relations with interest groups and its openness to interest group litigation. The Court clashed with interest groups in the mid-1980s, most starkly in a debate over how the Court should approach interest group interveners. Although the Supreme Court engaged in breathtaking activism in its early Charter cases (Morton, Russell, Riddell 1995), it did little to make more room for interest group interveners in its cases. In fact, beginning in 1984, it began to clamp down on interest group participation in its cases. Groups that were eager to exploit their victories over the wording of the Charter found themselves frozen out of the process of interpreting the Charter. These groups and their academic supporters voiced their outrage at the Supreme Court's view of the role groups should play in Charter adjudication. This criticism posed a serious threat to the Court's legitimacy just as the Court was starting to overturn legislation and censure police actions under the Charter.

In early 1983, the Supreme Court approved a new set of procedural rules, including an overhaul of its rules on intervention.[17] For seventy-five years between 1907 and 1983, the Supreme Court had not once changed its Rule 60 on intervention, so it was natural for the new rules to attract attention.[18] The timing of the new rules—just as the Charter era was getting under way—only drew heightened attention to the new rules. With the new rules, the Court looked as if it was welcoming interest group interveners in its work while trying to streamline the process of handling intervention applications. Under the old Rule 60, every would-be intervener had to apply to the Court to be heard. The new Rule 32 gave attorneys general the right to intervene in constitutional cases. The new Rule 18 also gave interveners who had intervened in a case before a lower court the right to intervene at the Supreme Court. Only new, nongovernment actors would need to apply for leave to intervene at the Supreme Court. This rule certainly sent a signal to the groups that were mobilizing for litigation that the Court was expanding the role they would play in its cases. As one CCLA vice-president later observed:

> Coming into force just as the first Charter appeals were reaching the Supreme Court of Canada, the new rule appeared to reinforce the welcome the court had given [to interest groups in the 1970s] . . . and seemed to suggest that the court shared the view that the advent of the Charter would require a more participatory adjudicative process to complement the court's new constitutional role. (Swan 1987, 32)

The new rules on intervention did not last through Christmas of that year, though. The first hint that the Court was rethinking its new approach came in November 1983. Justice Ritchie refused to allow the Ontario Association for the Mentally Retarded to intervene in the appeal of *R v Ogg-Moss*, a criminal case regarding the disciplining of children. In announcing his decision, Ritchie went on to proclaim that interveners in lower courts would no longer have the right to intervene in the Supreme Court in criminal cases.[19] A few weeks later, less than a year after the new rules came into effect, the Court rescinded the automatic right of interveners at lower courts to intervene at the Supreme Court altogether.[20] After seventy-six years with the same rules on interveners, the Supreme Court changed the rules three times in 1983.

The Court's change of rules at the end of 1983 marked the beginning of a new trend. Would-be interest group interveners began to be turned away. Groups that were mobilizing litigation to emulate the NAACP or the ACLU found they were losing a good way to get before the Supreme Court. Since there was no formal avenue for these groups to lobby the Court quietly, they started a remarkable, unprecedented public campaign to make their views known to the Court.[21] In 1984, Alan Borovoy, the general counsel of the CCLA, wrote an open letter to the Court urging the judges to accept more interventions (1984). Jillian Welch published a law review article attacking the Court for having a view of interest group intervention "which is curiously out of step with the Charter's mandate to the Court" (Welch 1985, 204). Her article sounded the alarm on behalf of disadvantaged groups: "[E]xcluding interest groups from the litigation of 'public' issues will inevitably result in excluding the voices of minorities" (Welch 1985, 230). A CCLA vice-president appeared at an academic conference in early 1986 and blasted the Court for clamping down on interveners when it had broadened the rules of standing in constitutional cases (Swan 1987). An activist with the BC Civil Liberties Association published an extensive criticism of the Court's track record on intervention (Bryden 1987). One journalistic account later reported there had been "an outcry from the legal profession" over the Court's treatment of interest groups.[22]

The Supreme Court had rarely faced such blunt, public criticism. Once the Court made it clear that it would use its powers of judicial review under the Charter actively, it made its decisions on matters such as intervention salient to a variety of groups. Yet, without the support of the interest groups that were hurling this criticism at the Court, the Court could face a serious challenge to its legitimacy. The Court's judges responded with an unprecedented formal consultation with the groups that it had angered. In 1986, they asked the Canadian Bar Association's Supreme Court Liaison Committee to investigate the issue of interest group intervention and recommend a new policy to the Court. While this kind of stakeholder consultation is normal for government departments, agencies, and political parties, it was an innovation for the Court, which was unaccustomed to having stakeholders. The Canadian Bar Association Committee gave the groups that had criticized the Court an opportunity to mobilize a formal lobbying campaign. It received submissions from the CCLA, LEAF, the British Columbia Civil Liberties Association, and the Ontario Public Interest Advocacy Centre. All these submissions advocated a more permissive policy on interveners.[23] The CCLA brief claimed that "the Supreme Court of Canada should develop a rule on interventions which broadens the effective right of constituencies other than the immediate parties to participate in important public interest litigation" (Borovoy 1984, 6). It argued that a "liberal rule for the inclusion of such [interveners'] briefs would broaden the right to participate and permit the judges to obtain an ever expanding amount of assistance . . ." (Borovoy 1984, 6). At about the same time, a vice-president of the CCLA wondered before an academic audience why the Court had shut off such a bountiful source of information. "[O]ne would have thought that our judges would have welcomed all the help they could get" (Swan 1987, 27). For its part, LEAF explicitly saw the Court's treatment of interest groups through the lens of the political disadvantage theory. The traditional two party model cannot bind public interest litigation, according to its submission.

> A rule restricting participation to the parties who first bring a court action will effectively deny the poor and disadvantaged sectors of society, who are least able to initiate the litigation themselves, access to a process which will have a significant impact on their rights. (LEAF 1986, 3)

LEAF cited figures from O'Connor and Epstein (1981) to show how common amici curiae were at the U.S. Supreme Court (LEAF 1986, 8). The publication of Welch and Bryden's law review articles supported the lobby effort.

The CBA Committee met with Justices Estey, Chouinard, and McIntyre in October 1986, to recommend that the Court accept more interveners (Crane 1986). The Supreme Court responded with a new rule in May 1987.[24] To the disappointment of the groups involved in the consultation process, the new rules appeared on their face to be even harsher than the old one (Koch 1990, 162). They allowed the attorneys general to intervene by right in constitutional cases. All other would-be interveners would have to state their interest in an appeal in order to be heard. An applicant would have to show how its submissions were going to be useful to the Court and different from those of the other parties before it would be allowed to intervene. The new rules limited an intervener's factum to twenty pages and denied interveners the opportunity for oral argument before the Court without special leave. When the CCLA learned of the new rules, it appealed to the government to force the Court to accept more interveners. Borovoy wrote a "strongly worded" (Koch 1990,

162) letter to the minister of justice asking the government to force the Court to treat interveners more generously by amending the Supreme Court Act. Borovoy attached Welch's law review article to his letter, and complained that

> the evidence suggests rather strongly that the Court, without ceremony or consultation, has simply changed its policy [on interveners]. For reasons hitherto either unarticulated or only partly articulated, the Court has decided to be restrictive where once it was liberal. (Borovoy 1986, 3)

He also objected to the use of the CBA-Supreme Court Liaison Committee to redraft the rules. "The administration of justice must not be allowed to become the fiefdom of any elite group—judges or lawyers. . . . It is appropriate, therefore, to seek redress from the forum that is accountable to everyone—the Parliament of Canada" (Borovoy 1986, 5).

As it turns out, Borovoy and others who wanted the Court to accept more interveners need not have worried. The new rules marked the beginning of a thorough change in the Court's approach to intervention. Its treatment of applications for leave to intervene changed dramatically when the new rules came into effect. It started to grant almost all interest group applications for leave to intervene. The number of interventions the Court heard in Charter cases rose sharply. The next two sections of this chapter trace the statistical trends of the Court on leave to intervene applications and on total interventions. The figures show that since 1987, the Court has been quite receptive to interventions of almost all sorts.

APPLICATIONS FOR LEAVE TO INTERVENE: 1985–1999

The 1987 rules on intervention marked the beginning of a new approach to interveners at the Supreme Court. As Table 2.1 shows, the Court attracted only sporadic attention from interest groups from 1976 through 1983. Most of the requests to intervene came from attorneys general. There was only a handful of other inter-

**Table 2.1** Applications for Leave to Intervene, 1975–1999

| | Number of Applications | | Success Rates | |
| | | Non-Attorneys | | Non-Attorneys |
| Year | All Applicants | General | All Applicants | General |
| --- | --- | --- | --- | --- |
| 1976 | 0 | 0 | — | — |
| 1977 | 0 | 0 | — | — |
| 1978 | 8 | 0 | 100% | — |
| 1979 | 80 | 10 | 95% | 60% |
| 1980 | 60 | 9 | 97% | 78% |
| 1981 | 94 | 12 | 98% | 100% |
| 1982 | 99 | 16 | 94% | 63% |
| 1983 | 27 | 26 | 70% | 69% |
| 1984 | 40 | 29 | 65% | 52% |
| 1985 | 11 | 11 | 18% | 18% |
| 1986 | 14 | 11 | 57% | 64% |
| 1987 | 23 | 22 | 96% | 95% |
| 1988 | 42 | 37 | 86% | 89% |
| 1989 | 34 | 31 | 88% | 87% |
| 1990 | 30 | 24 | 83% | 79% |
| 1991 | 115 | 104 | 93% | 93% |
| 1992 | 29 | 27 | 79% | 81% |
| 1993 | 69 | 57 | 93% | 95% |
| 1994 | 84 | 66 | 92% | 91% |
| 1995 | 73 | 60 | 95% | 93% |
| 1996 | 139 | 125 | 96% | 96% |
| 1997 | 88 | 68 | 86% | 82% |
| 1998 | 98 | 69 | 95% | 93% |
| 1999 | 113 | 89 | 93% | 91% |
| Total | 774 | 425 | 89% | 83% |

*Source:* Supreme Court Bulletins, 1976–1984, 1993–1999; Supreme Court News, 1985–1993.

*Note:* In 1983, Attorneys General received the right to intervene in constitutional cases.

vention applications each year. When the first Charter cases arrived in 1983, the Court began to get applications from applicants other than the attorneys general. The Court accepted more than 69 percent of these applications in 1983. After the rule changes of 1983, the Court's acceptance rate for applications from groups and individuals dropped. It accepted fewer than 20 percent of leave to intervene applications in 1985. Yet, the major lobbying campaign by the CCLA and LEAF led to a sharp increase in both the number of applications and in the success rates for applications starting in 1987. That year, the Court accepted about 95 percent of the applications it decided. The number of applications in Charter cases from non-attorneys general more than tripled from 1986 to 1987, and such applications in Charter and other cases usually succeeded. Since 1987, many interest groups have applied for leave to intervene each year, and they have generally succeeded. The Court appears to have heeded the pressure for more interveners.

Table 2.2 shows the "club" of frequent applicants at the Supreme Court. Even the high aggregate success rates in Table 2.1 mask the 100 percent success rates of the Court's top applicants. The two principal advocates of a more open policy on interventions, the CCLA and LEAF, have been its biggest beneficiaries. LEAF has not been denied a single application for leave to intervene in seventeen tries.[25] The CCLA has not been refused leave to intervene since 1987. Most of the top applicants have enjoyed close to 100 percent success rates since 1987.

**Table 2.2** The Most Frequent Applicants for
Leave to Intervene, 1985–1999

| Applicant | # Applications | % Accepted |
|---|---|---|
| Attorney General of Canada | 44 | 98% |
| Attorney General for Ontario | 38 | 95% |
| Women's Legal Education and Action Fund (LEAF) | 29 | 100% |
| Canadian Civil Liberties Association | 20 | 95% |
| Attorney General of Quebec | 19 | 100% |
| Attorney General of British Columbia | 15 | 100% |
| Attorney General of Manitoba | 12 | 100% |
| Attorney General of Alberta | 12 | 100% |
| Criminal Lawyers' Association | 12 | 58% |
| Canadian Bar Association | 11 | 100% |

*Source:* The Supreme Court News, 1985–1993, Supreme Court Bulletins, 1993–1999.

How does the Court treat different types of applicants? Table 2.3 sorts the applications according to the broad type of applicant. Every type of applicant has had better than a 50 percent success rate between 1985 and 1999. Nonetheless, there are differences in the way the Court treats different types of would-be interveners. All types of governments are usually successful applicants, as are

**Table 2.3** Applications for Leave to Intervene
by Type of Applicant, 1985–1999

| Type of Applicant | #<br>Applications | %<br>Accepted |
|---|---|---|
| *Governments* | | |
| Attorney General of Canada | 44 | 98% |
| Provincial Attorneys General | 118 | 92% |
| Federal Agencies | 18 | 100% |
| Provincial Agencies | 61 | 93% |
| Local Governments | 26 | 100% |
| International Agencies | 2 | 100% |
| Subtotal | 269 | 95% |
| *Economic Interests* | | |
| Business Groups | 45 | 89% |
| Professional Groups | 121 | 95% |
| Unions | 29 | 72% |
| Corporations | 62 | 83% |
| Subtotal | 257 | 89% |
| *Citizen Groups* | | |
| Rights Groups | 113 | 96% |
| Language Groups | 20 | 94% |
| Environmental Groups | 18 | 100% |
| Ethnic Groups | 7 | 100% |
| Native Groups | 60 | 73% |
| Abortion Groups | 10 | 100% |
| Other Public Interest Groups | 60 | 92% |
| Religious Groups | 26 | 100% |
| Subtotal | 314 | 95% |
| *Individuals* | 81 | 65% |
| *Other Groups* | 39 | 90% |
| Total | 960 | 90% |

*Source:* Supreme Court News, 1985–1993, Supreme Court Bulletins, 1993–1999.
*Note:* Missing Data: 2.

**Table 2.4** Judicial Records Granting Leave to Intervene Applications, 1985–1999.

| Judge | Overall Record | | A-Gs | | Other Gov't | | Economic Ints | | Citizen Grps | | Individuals | |
|---|---|---|---|---|---|---|---|---|---|---|---|---|
| | # Heard | % Grnt'd | # Heard | % Grnt'd | # Heard | % Grnt'd | # Heard | % Grnt'd | # Heard | % Grnt'd | # Heard | % Grnt'd |
| Lamer | 58 | 90% | 10 | 100% | 7 | 100% | 13 | 85% | 19 | 84% | 9 | 89% |
| Cory | 78 | 91% | 12 | 92% | 18 | 100% | 6 | 100% | 22 | 100% | 11 | 64% |
| Sopinka | 62 | 92% | 7 | 86% | 4 | 100% | 11 | 91% | 32 | 100% | 6 | 50% |
| L'Heureux-Dubé | 115 | 95% | 10 | 100% | 9 | 100% | 34 | 100% | 41 | 95% | 15 | 73% |
| Iacobucci | 104 | 96% | 16 | 89% | 12 | 100% | 24 | 100% | 41 | 100% | 5 | 60% |
| Gonthier | 57 | 88% | 12 | 92% | 5 | 100% | 3 | 100% | 26 | 89% | 3 | 33% |
| McLachlin | 145 | 93% | 33 | 100% | 18 | 100% | 33 | 88% | 43 | 100% | 11 | 73% |
| LaForest | 130 | 86% | 10 | 80% | 4 | 100% | 91 | 89% | 18 | 89% | 7 | 43% |
| Bastarache | 57 | 82% | 22 | 100% | 1 | 0% | 12 | 42% | 21 | 90% | 0 | — |
| Binnie | 33 | 97% | 5 | 100% | 16 | 100% | 1 | 100% | 8 | 100% | 1 | 0% |
| Major | 59 | 100% | 15 | 100% | 6 | 100% | 15 | 100% | 20 | 100% | 0 | — |

*Source:* Supreme Court News, 1985–1993, Supreme Court Bulletins, 1993–1999.
*Note:* This table excludes judges deciding fewer than 30 applications. Missing data: 6.

business and professional groups. Most types of citizen interest groups fare quite well, with rights groups in particular faring about as well as attorneys general. This belies the criticism that the attorneys general are a class of preferred intervener.[26] Unions, native groups, and individual Canadians have had the most trouble getting into the Court's hearings. The fact that individuals are among the least welcome interveners at the Court demonstrates how much legal politics is for organized interests. The Court's openness to interveners has precious little to do with its treatment of individuals.[27] Table 2.3 may feed the criticism that the Court has not treated labor unions as favorably as other interests (Mandel 1989).

Quantitative studies of judicial decisions have stressed the systematic differences between individual judges in deciding the inherently contestable cases that involve the Charter (Heard 1991; Morton, Russell, Withey 1990; Morton, Russell, Riddell 1995). Judges also differ systematically in the authorities they cite in their reasons for judgment (Manfredi 1990). Since judges must issue written reasons when deciding cases, but only rarely issue reasons for deciding interveners' applications, judges have wider discretion to decide intervention applications. One might therefore expect even wider differences between judges in the way they handle leave to intervene applications. The evidence does not bear this out, however. As Table 2.4 shows, since 1985 most judges regularly approve 90–100 percent of the applications they hear. Judges are also remarkably consistent in how they handle the various kinds of applicants for leave to intervene.

Table 2.5 lists the cases that have attracted the most applications to intervene between 1985 and 1999.[28] Most of these top cases have been Charter cases, although the top two cases are not widely recognized as leading Charter cases. The *Nova Scotia Pharmacies* case attracted attention from many Quebec pharmacies. *Delgamuukw* raised a number of novel issues regarding aboriginal rights in Canada. Many aboriginal and business groups were interested in how the Court would settle these issues. The *Reference re: Firearms Act* attracted twelve groups of firearms owners and others interested in gun control. In these cases, the Court accepted nearly every group that applied to be heard. When a case that is of interest to many would-be interveners arrives at the Court, the Court is willing to hear from almost all of them.

**Table 2.5** Cases Attracting the Most Applications
for Leave to Intervene, 1985–1999.

| Case (Year of Applications) | Number of Applications | Number Accepted | Case Type |
|---|---|---|---|
| *Nova Scotia Pharmaceuticals* (1991) | 20 | 20 | Charter |
| *Delgamuukw* (1996) | 16 | 15 | Charter/ Indians |
| *Ref. Re: Firearms Act* (1999) | 14 | 14 | Division of Powers |
| *New Brunswick Broadcasting* (1992) | 13 | 13 | Charter |
| *Winnipeg Child and Family Services v. D.F.G.* (1996) | 12 | 12 | Charter |
| *Ref. Re: Sask. Electoral Boundaries* (1991) | 11 | 11 | Charter |
| *Stillman* (1996) | 11 | 11 | Charter |
| *Ref. Re: Remuneration of Provincial Court Judges* (1996) | 10 | 10 | Charter |
| *Mossop* (1991) | 10 | 10 | Charter/ Human Rights |
| *Rodriguez* (1993) | 10 | 10 | Charter |

*Source:* Supreme Court News, 1985–1993, Supreme Court Bulletins, 1993–1999.

The pattern in these numbers regarding the Court's treatment of interveners is clear. The Court has been more open to interveners since 1987, when the lobby campaign of the CCLA and other groups bore fruit. It has attracted an increasing number of applications to intervene, and granted more than 90 percent of them. A deeper look at the numbers uncovers additional interesting findings. First, the Court's most-frequent applicants are very successful in getting into court. Most types of applicants have had high success rates, with unions, individuals, and native groups having somewhat less success than others. The Court has generally treated applications from rights groups as well as those from governments. In addition, and contrary to what one might expect given the variety of judicial approaches to deciding substantive issues, there are few systematic differences in the way that each judge treats applications to intervene. Finally, in the cases that are interesting to the largest number of would-be interveners, the Court grants leave to almost every applicant.

INTERVENERS AT THE SUPREME COURT: 1984 TO 1999

The statistics on applications to intervene capture only part of the Court's changing treatment of interveners since the mid-1980s. The overall number of interventions is also an important measure. Table 2.6 shows the number of interveners in Charter cases decided by Supreme Court. It includes all the interveners listed in the Supreme Court Reports, whether they intervened automatically or

Table 2.6 Interventions in Charter Cases by Year, 1984–1999.

|       | Charter Cases | | | Number of Interveners | | | |
|-------|-------|-------------|------|-----------|-------|----------|-------|
|       |       | Number with |      | Attorneys | Other |          |       |
| Year  | Total | Interveners | %    | General   | Gov't | Nongov't | Total |
| 1984  | 4     | 3           | 75%  | 6         | 0     | 2        | 8     |
| 1985  | 11    | 6           | 55%  | 14        | 0     | 9        | 23    |
| 1986  | 11    | 7           | 64%  | 21        | 0     | 7        | 28    |
| 1987  | 25[a] | 12          | 48%  | 46        | 17    | 15       | 78    |
| 1988  | 25    | 17          | 68%  | 32        | 4     | 8        | 44    |
| 1989  | 30    | 12          | 40%  | 36        | 2     | 22       | 60    |
| 1990  | 45[b] | 23          | 51%  | 85        | 4     | 39       | 128   |
| 1991  | 30[c] | 20          | 67%  | 58        | 14    | 34       | 106   |
| 1992  | 26    | 21          | 81%  | 50        | 1     | 47       | 98    |
| 1993  | 41[d] | 25          | 61%  | 53        | 21    | 46       | 120   |
| 1994  | 24    | 13          | 54%  | 15        | 0     | 11       | 26    |
| 1995  | 28    | 17          | 61%  | 49        | 1     | 40       | 90    |
| 1996  | 43    | 21          | 49%  | 48        | 4     | 62       | 114   |
| 1997  | 21    | 11          | 52%  | 24        | 1     | 52       | 77    |
| 1998  | 18    | 10          | 56%  | 29        | 1     | 23       | 53    |
| 1999  | 16    | 12          | 75%  | 25        | 0     | 52       | 77    |
| Total | 398   | 230         | 58%  | 591       | 70    | 469      | 1130  |

*Source:* Supreme Court Reports, 1984–1993, Supreme Court Bulletins, 1993–1999.

*Notes:*

[a] *Wigglesworth, Trumbley and Pugh,* and *Trimm* are counted as three cases, not one.

[b] *Ref. re: Prostitution, Skinner* and *Stagnetta, McKinney, Cornell,* and *Douglas College;* and Keegstra and Andrews are counted as eight cases, not three.

[c] *Rommeo* and *Ratti* are counted as two cases, not one.

[d] *Mossop* counted as a Charter case.

had to apply to be heard. The Court's change of approach in the late 1980s shows up clearly in these figures. The Court had a dozen nongovernment interveners per year in the 1985–1988 period, but three to four dozen per year in the 1990–1993 period. Between 1990 and 1999 the Court heard an average of 1.4 nongovernment interveners in each Charter case compared to an average of 0.5 between 1985 and 1988. The Court was much more welcoming of interest groups by 1990, and has remained consistently welcoming since then.

Table 2.7 shows the most frequent interveners in Charter cases. Through the end of 1999, twenty-one interveners had participated in more than five of the Court's Charter cases. Governments dominate the list of Charter interveners, but both LEAF and the CCLA have surpassed the Newfoundland and Nova Scotia

**Table 2.7** The Most Frequent Interveners
in Charter Cases, 1984–1999

|  | Intervener | Number of Interventions |
|---|---|---|
| 1 | Attorney General of Canada | 126 |
| 2 | Attorney General of Quebec | 106 |
| 3 | Attorney General for Ontario | 101 |
| 4 | Attorney General of Alberta | 54 |
| 5 | Attorney General of British Columbia | 52 |
| 6 | Attorney General of Manitoba | 47 |
| 7 | Attorney General of Saskatchewan | 44 |
| 8 | Attorney General of New Brunswick | 24 |
| 9 | Women's Legal Education and Action Fund (LEAF) | 19 |
| 10 | Canadian Civil Liberties Association | 18 |
| 11 | Attorney General of Newfoundland | 15 |
| 12 | Attorney General of Nova Scotia | 13 |
| 13 | League for Human Rights of the B'Nai Brith | 9 |
| 14 | Canadian Jewish Congress | 8 |
| 15 | Charter Committee on Poverty Issues | 7 |
| 16 | British Columbia Wildlife Federation | 6 |
| 17 | Canadian Labour Congress | 6 |
| 18 | Fisheries Council of British Columbia | 6 |
| 19 | Criminal Lawyers' Association | 6 |
| 20 | Canadian Mental Health Association | 6 |
| 21 | Alliance Quebec | 6 |

*Source:* Supreme Court Reports, 1984–1993, Supreme Court Bulletins 1993–1999.

governments on the list. LEAF and the CCLA are the top non-government interveners. The League for Human Rights of the B'Nai Brith and the Canadian Jewish Congress, groups with experience in the Court's hate literature and war crimes cases, have also appeared frequently before the Supreme Court.

Table 2.8 counts interventions by type of intervener. While governments again dominate the intervener mechanism in Charter cases, various "citizen" or public interest groups make up one-fifth

**Table 2.8** Interveners in Charter Cases
by Type of Intervener, 1984–1999

| Type of Intervener | Number of Interventions | Percent of Total Interventions |
|---|---|---|
| *Governments* | | |
| Attorney General of Canada | 126 | |
| Provincial Attorneys General | 465 | |
| Federal Agencies | 9 | |
| Provincial Agencies | 22 | |
| Local Government | 43 | |
| International Government | 2 | |
| Subtotal | 667 | 59% |
| *Economic Interests* | | |
| Business Organizations | 40 | |
| Unions | 21 | |
| Professional Organizations | 48 | |
| Corporations | 24 | |
| Subtotal | 133 | 12% |
| *Public Interests* | | |
| Rights Organizations | 87 | |
| Language Groups | 29 | |
| Environmental Groups | 8 | |
| Ethnic Groups | 12 | |
| Native Groups | 34 | |
| Abortion Groups | 6 | |
| Other Groups | 46 | |
| Religious Groups | 22 | |
| Subtotal | 244 | 21% |
| *Individuals* | 70 | 6% |
| *Other Groups* | 16 | 1% |
| Total | 1130 | 100% |

*Source:* Supreme Court Reports, 1984–1993, Supreme Court Bulletins, 1993–1999.

of the intervener appearances. Rights groups such as LEAF and the CCLA are the most common citizen groups to appear. Language groups also intervene often, an indication of how important language rights cases are to the Court's Charter docket. Surprisingly, economic interests, even organized groups of economic interests, constitute rather few of the interventions before the Court. There are particularly few unions involved. Nonetheless, the Court has heard from a variety of groups and interests in Charter cases.

Table 2.9 breaks down interventions according to which side of the case the intervener supported. Did the intervener support

Table 2.9 Types of Interveners and Side Supported
in Charter Cases, 1984–1999

| | Attorneys General | | | Other Government Officials | | | Nongovernment Interveners | | |
|---|---|---|---|---|---|---|---|---|---|
| Year | RC | N | ~RC | RC | N | ~RC | RC | N | ~RC |
| 1984 | 2 | 0 | 4 | 0 | 0 | 0 | 1 | 0 | 1 |
| 1985 | 0 | 0 | 14 | 0 | 0 | 0 | 9 | 0 | 0 |
| 1986 | 3 | 0 | 18 | 0 | 0 | 0 | 7 | 0 | 0 |
| 1987 | 2 | 0 | 44 | 4 | 0 | 13 | 10 | 0 | 5 |
| 1988 | 7 | 0 | 25 | 0 | 0 | 4 | 3 | 0 | 5 |
| 1989 | 1 | 4 | 31 | 0 | 0 | 2 | 6 | 5 | 11 |
| 1990 | 4 | 3 | 78 | 2 | 0 | 2 | 12 | 1 | 26 |
| 1991 | 2 | 0 | 56 | 3 | 0 | 6 | 24 | 0 | 7 |
| 1992 | 3 | 0 | 47 | 0 | 0 | 1 | 42 | 0 | 5 |
| 1993 | 1 | 0 | 52 | 6 | 2 | 13 | 22 | 1 | 19 |
| 1994 | 0 | 3 | 11 | 0 | 0 | 7 | 4 | 0 | 0 |
| 1995 | 0 | 0 | 49 | 1 | 9 | 10 | 21 | 0 | 0 |
| 1996 | 0 | 4 | 42 | 0 | 0 | 4 | 44 | 0 | 17 |
| 1997 | 0 | 7 | 17 | 0 | 0 | 1 | 37 | 3 | 12 |
| 1998 | 0 | 9 | 20 | 1 | 0 | 0 | 17 | 0 | 6 |
| 1999 | 0 | 0 | 24 | 0 | 0 | 0 | 40 | 0 | 10 |
| Total | 25 | 30 | 532 | 17 | 11 | 63 | 299 | 10 | 124 |
| | | 587 | | | 91 | | | 433 | |
| | | | | 1111 | | | | | |

*Sources:* Interveners' factums, archives of the Supreme Court of Canada, Ottawa, Supreme Court Reports, 1984–1993, Supreme Court Bulletins, 1993–1999.

*Notes:* Missing data: 19.
RC — Supports Rights Claim
N — Takes No Position on Rights Claim
~RC — Opposes Rights Claim

the rights claimant or oppose the rights claimant? This table provides a fascinating set of results. While one might think that all governments intervene against rights claims and that interest groups intervene to support rights claims, this is not the case. Most interventions by the attorneys general do oppose the rights claimant, but an important minority of these interventions support the rights claimant. Moreover, one in five interventions by other government officials support the rights claimant. Nongovernment interveners have an even more mixed record. Most nongovernment interveners support the party claiming a Charter right, but almost one-third of them oppose the party claiming the Charter right. During these years even rights groups, who might be expected to support Charter claims consistently, support the government side and oppose the rights claim in about one-third of their interventions. Therefore, it is too simple to see Charter cases as pitting governments on one side against rights claims and nongovernment interveners on the other. Instead, as Table 2.9 shows, both government and nongovernment interveners appear on both sides of Charter cases.

## CONCLUSION

Since the Supreme Court's role in Canada's system of government began to change in the 1970s, the Court has also changed the role of interest groups in its work. This can be seen clearly in its new treatment of interveners. In the mid-1980s, the Court came under heavy criticism by interest groups and legal commentators who wanted the Court to accept many more interventions. Their lobbying campaign was brilliantly successful. Whereas the Supreme Court was relatively reluctant to hear interveners from 1984 to 1986, it has heard almost all would-be interveners since 1987.

Why did the Court adopt the position of the lobbyists so decisively? The interest groups and commentators involved wanted to exert as much influence over the Court as possible. Why did the Court go along with them? It is important to recall the broader background to this development. During the early and mid-1980s the Supreme Court used its power of judicial review more actively than it ever had before. It staked out bold new ground using the

Charter, placing no significant limits on its own powers to review government actions and replace the judgment of government officials with its own. No court can do such a thing for long without the support of political interests. Just as the Trudeau government found civil liberties and rights oriented groups useful allies for legitimating its patriation project, so the Supreme Court found these groups to be useful allies in legitimating its extraordinary activism. By accommodating interest groups, the Court blunted their potentially damaging criticism. Allying itself with "disadvantaged groups" furthermore provided a justification for what otherwise might appear to be an unconscionable power grab. The next chapter turns to these issues.

# 3

# INTEREST GROUP LITIGATION
# AND JUDICIAL SUPREMACY

The Supreme Court of Canada's change in approach to interest group intervention was more than a matter of numbers. The Court did more than just bend to pressure from interest groups to allow more interveners in its cases. It also changed its doctrine on intervention, and in setting out this new doctrine, it was working out a new role for itself in Canada's constitutional order. In the 1950s and 1960s, the Court saw itself primarily as an adjudicative institution. It therefore had little reason to open the judicial system's doors to interest groups litigation. In the 1970s, the Supreme Court embraced Trudeau's program of reform to become a creative, reform-oriented law-making institution. A law-making court can benefit from the involvement of interest groups in its cases, and so the Supreme Court began to hear from interest group interveners. When the Court began to grapple with Charter cases in the mid-1980s, it took a step beyond simply being one law-making institution among many in the Canadian constitutional order. It claimed to be the country's supreme interpreter of constitutional law.

Claims to judicial supremacy need to be carefully justified in a democratic country. In the early years of the Charter, the Court opted for the legalistic defense of its claim to judicial supremacy. The legalistic defense of judicial supremacy leaves little room for interest group intervention, and this might explain the Court's clampdown. In any case, legal commentators writing in law reviews and other legal publications criticized the Court for this clampdown, as outlined in the previous chapter. In doing so, they urged the Court to recognize that its role was political, and accept more interest group interveners. However, the more political view of judicial supremacy that the commentators advocated put the Court in a conundrum. If the Court's role is a political rather than a legal one, why should its interpretations of the constitution trump those of other political institutions? Why should it be able to strike down legislation, or invalidate actions of the government?

The concept of the disadvantaged group solved this conundrum for the Court. Its claims that judges must be the supreme interpreters of Canada's constitutional law would have been nothing more than institutional arrogance or pretense without a careful justification. Other political actors would have quickly beaten back this judicial power grab unless the Court had a plausible reason for needing the power it grabbed. The concept of the disadvantaged group provides a reason for judicial supremacy. Why must judges have the final say in the development of constitutional law, even in a democratic country? Because other government institutions cannot do justice for some groups in society. Some groups are shut out of, or at least disadvantaged in, the cabinet, the bureaucracy, and executive federalism (the legislative and executive branches of government, in the American version of the argument). If their rights and interests are to be respected, the courts must act on their behalf.

If judicial supremacy needs the concept of the disadvantaged group, disadvantaged groups also need judicial supremacy. Judicial supremacy ensures that the courts can uphold their rights and interests. Disadvantaged groups cannot depend on traditional, English-style adjudication to vindicate their rights. The adjudicative model of judging focuses too narrowly on resolving concrete legal disputes. Disadvantaged groups must have courts that take on a creative role in making law, and the supreme role in interpreting and enforcing constitutional law. A judiciary that can rise above the other institutions of government can do justice on behalf of the disadvantaged.

This chapter begins by looking at the adjudicative era of the Supreme Court's history, and the limited role interest group intervention played in its work during these years. It then turns to the Trudeau government's judicial reforms of the 1970s. It shows how these reforms were intended to move the Supreme Court away from its traditional adjudicative role toward a law-making role. Next, the analysis turns to the Charter era. The Court took up the Charter's challenge to lay claim to supremacy in the interpretation of constitutional law, but it also clamped down on the number of interveners it heard. This clampdown has often been attributed to the severe workload problems the Court was experiencing at the time, but the Court's treatment of interveners also followed from its legalistic justification for judicial supremacy. The chapter then details the criticisms that legal commentators have leveled at the Court's treatment of interest group interveners. They criticized the Court's legalism and feared it would lead the Court back to its previous emphasis on adjudication. Legal commentators acting as advocates rather than mere analysts warned the Court that it would face a crisis of legitimacy if it continued to turn away interest groups, especially politically disadvantaged groups. In the end, the Supreme Court changed its approach and began accepting many interveners. At the same time, in a series of written reasons in leave to intervene applications, Justice Sopinka rewrote the Court's rules on intervention to conform to the requirements of a political version of judicial supremacy. The new judicial role that is inherent in the Court's new approach to interest group intervention raises serious problems, though. The Court cannot admit its political role or it would face a loss in its legitimacy.

## The Adjudicative Supreme Court of Canada

In the course of resolving concrete legal disputes between the parties to those disputes, every court makes new law, because every court must interpret the law. Courts differ, though, in whether they see a case primarily as an opportunity to resolve a dispute or an opportunity to make new law. In effect, there is a spectrum of possible judicial roles. At the "adjudicative" end of the spectrum, courts focus on resolving individual, concrete legal disputes and pay less heed to their law-making role. At the "law making" end of the spectrum, courts see individual, concrete legal disputes merely as vehicles for engaging in creative law making (Knopff and Morton 1992, Chapter 7; Weiler 1968). This distinction matters. The adjudicative court has an inherently limited role. It does not devote its resources to cases simply for the opportunities they afford for making new law. The law-making court does not accept such limits on its work. Adjudicative and law-making courts approach questions of interest group litigation, intervention, and standing in much different ways.

For most of its first century, the Supreme Court saw its primary role as adjudicating concrete legal disputes. Even after Canada abolished appeals to the Judicial Committee of the Privy Council in 1949, its judges still clung to English legal precedents. By "treating the common law as a closed book the judges could deny themselves a creative role in adapting the law to contemporary Canadian circumstances" (Russell 1987, 341). There were aspects of the Court's work that went beyond simple adjudication. As an appeals court, it made new law whenever it decided a case involving unsettled legal issues. The Canadian reference mechanism, which allows the federal cabinet to ask the Court hypothetical questions, forces the Court to make law without having a concrete legal dispute before it. The Court also decided cases about the federal-provincial division of powers. This implicitly made the Court a referee between the two levels of government. Yet, despite these nonadjudicative aspects to its work, the Court tried to stick as closely to traditional appellate adjudication as it could. The Court was staffed with traditional judges who were usually content to hew closely to the traditionalist British model of a common law court of appeals. Most cases appeared before the Court by right, so the judges had little control over their docket. As long as it was staffed by tradition-minded judges and had no control over its own docket, the Supreme Court was content to focus on resolving concrete legal disputes.

An adjudicative court has little need for interest group litigation. So, it is not surprising that the Supreme Court gave Canadian interest groups little attention during this period in its history. It kept Canada's law of standing restrictive, so only individuals or corporations involved in concrete legal disputes could sue. Letting others launch lawsuits would have involved the courts in nonadjudicative business. The focus on adjudication also limited the Court's ability to accept interveners. An adjudicative court can depend on the parties to bring any relevant information to its attention (Horowitz 1977; Weiler 1968). There is no need for any wider perspectives or additional arguments. The traditional Canadian rules on intervention reflected the adjudicative view of the judicial function. Until the Charter era, Canadian courts used a two-pronged test to decide applications to intervene. First, a would-be intervener had to demonstrate an interest in a case, usually an economic interest in the specific outcome of the dispute and not just an interest in the precedent to be set (Welch 1985, 210–211). Secondly, a would-be intervener had to show that the parties to the case would not adequately represent its interest. These were difficult standards to meet, and they excluded most interest groups from intervening. Moreover, interveners would not be heard in two special situations. No one could intervene in a case just because he or she was a party in a case on the same point of law before a lower court. Since the Court shied away from acknowledging a law-making role for itself, it depended on the parties to each case to bring all the relevant arguments to court. As one commentator noted, "there is little to be said for attempting to resolve one's own legal dispute in the procedural context of someone else's lawsuit" (Bryden 1987, 499). Interveners were also not generally heard where they would widen the scope of the legal dispute (the *lis*) between the parties. An intervener "must accept the parameters of the case as defined by the parties . . . " (Scriven and Muldoon 1985, 459). An adjudicative court resolves the dispute between the parties to a case, not the dispute that an intervener would like to have heard. In reference cases, which usually lack an adjudicative context, the courts heard interveners more readily, but in most instances these rules made intervention rare. When interveners were heard they had little room to stray from the confines of the immediate case.

## RETOOLING THE SUPREME COURT

As chapter 2 notes, in the early and mid-1970s the Trudeau government embarked on a series of judicial reforms. Trudeau's objective was to change the judiciary's role in Canada's constitutional order, moving it away from strict adherence to the adjudicative ideal of judging. He wanted the courts to pay as much attention to creative law making as to resolving concrete legal disputes. As the previous chapter noted, he thought more judicial law making would promote the kind of modernizing law reform he needed to make Canada a just society, "updating" Canadian law to take account of new social realities. Moving the courts toward more of a law-making role would also augment the power of a national institution. This factor became important to Trudeau as Quebec separatism gained strength in the 1970s, as chapter 5 discusses at greater length. As the last chapter noted, Trudeau's judicial reform program involved two changes for the Supreme Court. First, he appointed a new generation of more scholarly and activist judges to the bench. Equally importantly, Parliament amended the Supreme Court Act in 1974 to give the Court more control over its own docket. The Court was told to hear only cases that involved matters "of public importance." This, it was hoped, would free the Court from the work of deciding routine commercial cases. These twin reforms—the appointment of a new generation of judges and giving the Court control over its docket—allowed the Court to shift its attention away from adjudication and toward law making.

The shift in the Court's role meant a corresponding change in the Court's relationship with interest groups. An adjudicative court has little need for interest groups, but a law-making court usually relies on groups to participate actively in its work. It must, for example, change its approach to interveners. When law making becomes a court's central focus, it cannot trust the parties to a case to bring forward all the types of information that it needs. "[I]f the essence of judicial decision-making is the formulation of general policy for society, all those whose positions are affected by the policy have an interest in the best possible argument being made to the court" (Weiler 1968, 445–446). When a court gets involved in wider law-making questions, interveners are needed "to get before the court those considerations that are relevant to the interests of other affected parties" (1968: 449). A shift toward greater law making also has implications for the law of standing. Restrictive rules of standing keep some questions out of court. A court that fully embraces a law making role must loosen the rules of standing, to allow all kinds of legal issues to find their way into the judiciary. As the Supreme Court took on a wider role, it needed a new approach to interest group intervention and the law of standing.

As the previous chapter noted, the Supreme Court first indicated that its new constitutional role would mean a new relationship with interest groups in the *Lavell* (1974) and *Morgentaler* (1976) cases. By allowing groups to intervene in these cases, the Court acknowledged that its decisions in these cases would have an impact beyond the immediate parties. The Court was going to engage in creative law reform, so it needed to hear from any groups that would be affected by its work. This advertised the Court's acceptance of a new law-making role. The Court followed up on *Lavell* and *Morgentaler* when it loosened the rules of standing in *Thorson* (1975), *McNeil* (1976), and *Borowski* (1981). These cases effectively expanded the number of legal issues that could be raised in court and expanded the opportunities for interest group litigation. It allowed citizens and groups to challenge legislation when their only interest was of a general concern for the law's validity where there is "no other reasonable and effective manner in which the issue may be brought before the Court" (*Borowski* 1981, 576). No longer would the courts strike out cases simply because they did not meet traditional rules of standing. Every law could be subject to a constitutional challenge, and thus subject to being rewritten by the Supreme Court. If no concrete dispute could arise that would question a law's constitutionality, any individual or interest group would be able to launch a challenge. The cumulative effect of these decisions—to hear interveners in *Lavell* and *Morgentaler,* and then to change Canada's rules of standing in *Thorson*, *McNeil,* and *Borowski*—did not merely graft new and more permissive rules about interest group litigation onto the Court's traditional work. Rather, they indicated that the Court was accepting Trudeau's invitation to choose a new constitutional role for itself. It was laying a claim to a role in creative law making. No longer would the Court be restricted to a traditional, English-style adjudicative idea of what judging properly entailed. The Court would put law making in the forefront of its concerns.

These developments got an enthusiastic response. Bernard Dickens, a prominent law professor at the University of Toronto and one of Laskin's former colleagues, praised Laskin for adopting an American approach to amici curiae in *Lavell* and *Morgentaler*. The two cases pointed to "the emergence of an authentic North American procedural jurisprudence uniting Canada and the United States of America" on interest group intervention, he wrote (Dickens 1977, 666). He noted that during his academic career Laskin had urged the Supreme Court to take on a law-making role. Dickens hoped that as chief justice, Laskin would move the Court toward the U.S. Supreme Court's style of law reform. He linked the new approach to interest group intervention to the protection of vulnerable minorities. "In the United States," he wrote, "the amicus curiae has come to enjoy a distinguished twentieth-century history in the promotion of minority interests . . ." (672). Canada had seen the emergence of "comparable activist groups" such as the CCLA, feminist groups, ethnic groups, and Indian rights groups. Presumably, they would push the Supreme Court of Canada to take a more active law-making role as well. The Court's reworking of the law of standing got a similar reaction from legal commentators (McCalla 1980; Evans 1981; Chester 1983; Tokar 1984). This commentary demonstrated that as the Court changed its role in the Canadian political order, it would have the support of leading legal commentators.

## INTO THE CHARTER ERA

The 1982 constitutional amendments were designed, in part, to encourage the Supreme Court to go beyond a law-making role. A law-making court may see itself as simply one among many law-making institutions in a country. The 1982 package of constitutional reforms held out the promise of an even more prominent position. Several of the amendments were designed to let the Court claim the supreme role in making constitutional law. Section 52 of the 1982 Constitution Act explicitly established the supremacy of constitutional law over government actions.[1] Section 24 of the new Charter authorized judges to take the supreme role in enforcing the Charter.[2] As Knopff and Morton point out, even the wording of the Charter's "notwithstanding" clause, which allows legislatures to reenact laws that violate judicial interpretations of the Charter, accepts the idea that the Charter is what the judges say it is. "[I]t assumes that section 33 can only be used only to override rights as defined by judges rather than to express an alternative interpretation of those rights" (Knopff and Morton 1992, 179). Almost the entire package of constitutional amendments urged the Court to take on the supreme role in making constitutional law. The Court would not need to see itself as one law-making authority among many. It could claim the lead role, and use the constitution to trump the law making of the other branches of government.

The Court responded to the Charter by taking full advantage of its mandate to judicial supremacy. It could have refused to use the Charter to the fullest, just as it refused to use the 1960 Bill of Rights to engage in more active judicial review. It could have seen the Charter as simply adding to the "legal background against which judges resolve concrete disputes" (Knopff and Morton 1992, 180). Rather than decline the Charter's invitation to claim supremacy in constitutional law making, it accepted the invitation fully. In its early Charter cases, it made its intentions clear in grandiose statements. In *Skapinker* (1984), its very first Charter case, Justice Estey made it clear that the Court would claim supremacy in the interpretation of the Charter. The 1982 constitutional reforms, he wrote, added "a new yardstick of reconciliation between the individual and the community and their respective rights, a dimension which, like the balance of the Constitution, remains to be interpreted and applied by the Court" (*Skapinker* 1984, 366–367). He appealed to the U.S. experience by quoting Chief Justice Marshall's words in *Marbury* (1803), the first case in which the U.S. Supreme Court claimed to be supreme in interpreting the U.S. Constitution.

> It is emphatically the province and duty of the judicial department to say what the law is. . . . So if a law be in opposition to the constitution . . . the courts must determine which of these conflicting rules governs the case. This is of the very essence of judicial duty. (177)

In *Operation Dismantle* (1985), the Court claimed its Charter interpretations could trump the cabinet's foreign policy decisions. A few months later, in the *Reference re: BC Motor Vehicles Act*

(1985), Justice Lamer dismissed concerns about judicial supremacy. He wrote: "[T]he courts are empowered, indeed required, to measure the content of legislation against the guarantees of the constitution" (496). This line of reasoning culminated in *BC Government Employees Union* (1988), when the Court ruled that picketing a courthouse interferes with access to the courts, "that which alone makes it in fact possible to benefit" from the Charter. Chief Justice Dickson concluded that without unhindered access to the courts, "the Charter protections would become merely illusory, the entire Charter undermined" (1988, 229).

In claiming supremacy in the interpretation of Canadian constitutional law, the Court also engaged in a blistering round of judicial activism. In its first two years of Charter cases, the Court sided with the rights claimant in 64 percent of its Charter decisions (Morton, Russell, and Riddell, 1995, 3). Over the next seven years, its activism subsided and it sided with the rights claimant in between 23 percent and 38 percent of its Charter cases. Morton, Russell, and Riddell argue that this drop in activism came as the Court's "Charter honeymoon" ended and the judges began to grapple with the contentious nature of their new job (Morton, Russell, and Riddell, 1995, 6–7). It is also possible that the Court's early rate of supporting rights claimants encouraged more marginal cases to come forward. Regardless, in its first decade deciding Charter cases, the Court pursued a much more active course than it had ever pursued before. It rewrote Canadian criminal, administrative, language, and aboriginal law. From 1982 to 1989, it struck down eight federal and eleven provincial laws, for a total of nineteen (Morton, Russell, and Withey 1992, 25).

The Supreme Court accepted the 1982 Constitution Act's invitation to claim supremacy in interpreting constitutional law, but it disappointed the interest groups that expected to be heard before the Court. These groups thought that if the Court claimed the supreme role in interpreting the Constitution, it would expand the role of interest groups in its work. As chapter 2 notes, the Court instead clamped down on interest group interveners and provoked public criticism from the groups that were mobilizing legal action. Most scholars attribute this clampdown to the need to streamline the Court's work and clear the large backlog of cases that the Court faced in the mid-1980s. In 1987, for example,

Peter Russell explained: "In response to the severe workload problems it has been experiencing in the early years of the Charter, the Supreme Court has cut down severely on interventions by public interest groups" (Russell 1987, 353). This explanation could well be correct. The Court had accumulated a serious backlog of cases by the mid-1980s. It was seriously short of active judges. Laskin was in ill health during his last years on the Court and was frequently absent. Estey took a leave of absence in 1985 to chair a commission of inquiry into the collapse of two western Canadian banks and left the Court short another judge. Ritchie retired in October 1984 and was not replaced by LaForest until mid-January 1985. Chouinard died in February 1987 and was not replaced by L'Heureux-Dubé until April of that year. The fact that the clampdown on interveners coincided with the Supreme Court's determined efforts to clear its backlog certainly implies that the Court cut back on the number of interveners as a way of getting though cases more quickly.

Another possible explanation is that the Court's reluctance to hear interveners in these early Charter years also flowed from its own conception of judicial supremacy. Judicial supremacy is hard to justify in a democratic regime. There are two very different arguments to justify it. One is a legalistic argument. It claims that the courts can take the lead role in interpreting and enforcing the Constitution because this role is not a creative one. According to the legalistic version of judicial supremacy, the courts do not make law when they interpret the Constitution. They are engaged in a mechanical process of "discovering" principles of constitutional law that already exist in the document itself. The judicial role is "rationally discerning the logical implications of agreed upon legal principles in situations where more politically-sensitive institutions are likely to be distracted by interests and passions" (Knopff and Morton 1992, 196). The second argument for judicial supremacy acknowledges that interpreting the constitution is inherently creative and involves a court in inherently political disputes. According to the political version of judicial supremacy, a court should embrace its political role as a way of compensating for inadequate checks and balances in the legislative and executive branches. Given the weakness of bicameralism and the strong party discipline in Canadian legislatures, this is always a powerful argument. Courts can claim supremacy because they must check an overly powerful prime minister and cabinet (Knopff and Morton 1992, chapter 8).

The Supreme Court opted for the legalistic defense of its role under the Charter in its early cases. It denied that it was in any way "making" law when it engaged in judicial review under the Charter. Instead, it claimed to be judging legislation and government action against clear principles of constitutional law. Judicial supremacy, in the Court's view, involved the mechanical application of constitutional law to subordinate forms of law. In short, the Court's role was not creative at all. In *re: the BC Motor Vehicles Act*, Lamer responded to criticisms that the Court was becoming a "superlegislature" in its Charter cases:

> It ought not to be forgotten that the historic decision to entrench the Charter in our Constitution was taken not by the courts but by the elected representatives of the people of Canada. It was those representatives who extended the scope of constitutional adjudication and entrusted the courts with this new and onerous responsibility. Adjudication under the Charter must be approached free of any lingering doubts as to its legitimacy. (1985: 497)

The legalistic defense of judicial supremacy leaves only narrow grounds for interest group intervention. If judicial review under the Constitution is a purely legalistic exercise, then interveners are not essential to a court's work. The judicial role is simply to use constitutional principles to determine whether a piece of legislation is valid. There is generally no need for judges to consider the positions of various interest groups on that question. If interest group interveners might broaden the range of legal arguments before a court and therefore increase the likelihood of the court picking the correct answer to the question before it, intervention is acceptable. Dickens advanced a version of this argument before the advent of the Charter. "The risk of available judgments being overlooked by counsel and courts themselves," in busy court systems, "is such that courts, and parties with an interest in avoiding expensive appeals, are genuinely helped by counsel for motivated non-parties assisting the presentation of relevant precedents" (1977,

674–675). However, if a court has the services of a reasonably competent bar and law clerks, this is not much of a concern. The legalistic defense of judicial supremacy means interest group intervention should be rare.[3] It is possible that the Supreme Court of Canada's clampdown on interveners following from the Court's legalistic conception of its own role.

Regardless of the reason for the clampdown, the Court's reluctance to hear interveners provoked criticisms from legal commentators, just as it had provoked criticisms from the interest groups that were mobilizing for legal action. In the mid- and late 1980s, Canadian law journals published several articles that strongly criticized the Court's approach to intervention. These commentators were not simply academic analysts; they acted as advocates for the position that the Court should accept more interveners. They excoriated the Court for taking too legalistic a view of its role. They urged the Court to embrace a law-making role and to adopt the political version of judicial supremacy. The Supreme Court ended up responding to these criticisms in the late 1980s. To understand how much this commentary on intervention influenced the Court, it is useful to review the main elements of the commentary.

These commentators made a number of arguments about the Court's approach to intervention. They began by rejecting any legalistic view of the Supreme Court's role in the Charter era. They wanted the Supreme Court to pursue its claims of judicial supremacy, but they wanted the Court to see judicial supremacy in political, rather than legalistic, terms. Jillian Welch was the first to put forth this criticism. She based her argument for interest group intervention on the premise that "civil rights adjudication is an inherently political exercise that the court must perform, involving interests transcending those of the original parties" (1985, 228). The Charter "undeniably vests what are essentially political decisions in the hands of a non-elected judiciary" (228). Philip Bryden, an academic and an activist in the BC Civil Liberties Association, concurred. "Fundamental to the belief that public interest intervention is justified is the proposition that judges make law" (1987, 505). Sharon Lavine, writing a few years later, agreed and argued that the Charter, "has invited and indeed obliged the Court to engage in the type of inquiry and debate that traditionally was reserved to the political arena" (1992, 28). In the view of the commentators, since the courts' role under the Charter is inherently political they must hear from interest group interveners. The Supreme Court could not perform its law-making function without hearing from groups that had an interest in any new law the Court might make.

These commentators were also, not surprisingly, hostile to the adjudicative model of judging. They saw the Court's reluctance to hear interveners as an attempt to revert to its earlier adjudicative ways. They unanimously dismissed the adjudicative view of judging as arcane and outdated, certainly as far as the Supreme Court of Canada was concerned. Welch argued that the "traditional private law model of litigation" was "strained to the breaking point" by the kind of multipolar, public law cases that the Court had to grapple with (1985, 213). To her, the Court's "vision of a limited judicial role" was "oddly anachronistic" (231). She criticized the Court for thinking that its own role was "the adjudication of the legal rights of the parties to a dispute," rather than being "the arbiter of larger legal questions of social and economic import" (222–223). Bryden wrote that although the adjudicative model had "much to recommend it if the entire object of the exercise is the resolution of disputes," the Court's new role was much wider. Making law while resolving disputes "is a major part of the exercise" and the Court cannot simply rely on the parties to the dispute to present all the arguments and information the Court would need to make law. It must hear interest group interveners (1987, 514). A few years later, John Koch declared that the "traditional view of the court as a forum for dispute resolution between private parties" is "naive and obsolete in the light of the public implications of judicial decisions" (Koch 1990, 151). Lavine also criticized the adjudicative model because it "cannot provide an adequate forum for the resolution of the complex issues which arise in a modern welfare state" (1992, 30).

The commentators pressed the Court to realize that if it claimed the supreme role in constitutional interpretation, it should realize the political nature of its role and accept more interest group intervention. Hearing more interveners would put more information before the Court and lead to more informed decisions. Welch, for example, argued that, "the involvement of non-parties will necessarily ensure that a more comprehensive range of issues and remediable possibilities will be put before the court" (1985, 229). In Bryden's version of the argument, "a variety of inputs is likely to make for more informed and, one hopes, better judicial decision-making" (1987, 507). The commentators were particularly excited that interest group interveners would bring "Brandeis briefs" to court. One pair of commentators argued that in the United States preparing Brandeis briefs was one of the most important functions of the amicus curiae. These briefs "marshal sociological data, scientific and quasi-scientific facts designed to expand the general information basis for decision making" (Steel and Smith 1989, 67). Others wrote that amici "bring to the attention of the court background information (what are often described as 'legislative facts') that has revealed . . . the impact that a legal doctrine has on the people the group represents" (Bryden 1987, 507–508). Interveners' Brandeis briefs would help the Court make complex decisions in the full knowledge of their likely impact.[4]

The commentators also argued that accepting more interveners was a corollary to loosening the rules of standing. Looser rules of standing made strategic interest group litigation possible, and, "Strategic litigation by interest groups is impossible unless they can inject themselves into cases, brought by their interest 'opposites,' which would potentially cut down or alter, through precedent, their jurisprudential gains" (Welch 1985, 229). According to Bryden's version of the argument, since the Canadian Supreme Court had set weak barriers to standing, it had to allow interest groups to intervene in its cases.

> Broad access to the legal system for those who wish to raise legal issues of public importance brings with it the possibility that the issues will be presented . . . in a way that may be both rather abstract and excessively one-sided. . . . [I]t seems intuitively sensible that a person who has standing to raise an important issue by commencing a lawsuit should be able to make the same point by intervening in a lawsuit commenced by someone else. (1987, 512)

Kenneth Swan similarly linked the issue of intervention to the Court's liberalization of Canada's law of standing. Public interest litigation, he wrote, should not be "controlled entirely by the first interested citizen who happens along" (Swan 1987, 28).

Bolder commentators went beyond these arguments and warned the Court that it risked a crisis of legitimacy if it continued to turn away interest group interveners. Welch hinted that without more interveners, the Court could face an attack from disadvantaged groups. Excluding interest group interveners, she wrote, "will inevitably result in excluding the voices of minorities" (1985, 230). To make decisions in cases involving the rights of minorities without hearing from their representatives "is to leave these groups largely at the mercy of the majority and to discount their rights" (230). Swan, a CCLA vice-president, also roasted the Court for refusing to hear more interveners. He noted that amici representing disadvantaged groups had played an important role in the U.S. Supreme Court's work, and suggested that the CCLA would pursue more overt pressure tactics if the Canadian Supreme Court did not move on the intervention issue. Bryden, the BC Civil Liberties Association activist, argued that if interest groups were allowed to intervene in Supreme Court cases, they would be obligated to respect the Court's decisions. If interveners were shut out of the Court's work, their "legal obligation" to accept the Court's decision would remain, but their "moral obligation to do so will be subtly undermined." He continued with this warning to the Court: "And in a society in which the power of courts rests as much on their moral authority as on their ability to invoke the coercive power of the state, this is not a matter to be taken lightly" (1987, 510).

The thrust of this commentary was clear. For the commentators, the Court was right to claim the supreme role in constitutional interpretation, but wrong to see supremacy in legalistic terms. The commentators were not persuaded by the Court's legalistic defense of its work. They wanted the Court to see its role as creative and political, and to accept the responsibilities inherent in being political. A political court needs interest group intervention. The Court faced a difficult situation. If it did not accept more interest group interveners in its cases, it would face an attack on its legitimacy, an attack in the name of disadvantaged groups. A coalition of groups claiming to represent the disadvantaged in Canadian society, with the backing of legal commentators, would have hurt the Court's image in political and legal circles. But the Court's critics held out a bold alternative. If the Court accepted more of the right kind of interveners, disadvantaged groups would be drawn into its work. A mutually beneficial relationship between the Court and disadvantaged groups could protect the Court from attacks on its claim to be supreme in matters of constitutional law.

## THE SUPREME COURT SHIFTS ITS APPROACHES

As chapter 2 recounts, the Court finally responded to the concerted lobby campaign of groups such as the CCLA and began to accept more interest group interveners in 1987. But a quantitative analysis of the Court's track record does not fully describe the Court's new approach to interest group litigation. After 1987, once it had already begun to accept more interest group interveners, the Court issued a series of rare written reasons explaining why it granted or denied leave to intervene in a number of cases. In these written reasons, the Court signaled that it was responding to the legal commentators and changing gears, gradually abandoning the legalistic view of judicial supremacy and adopting a more political one.

Justice John Sopinka, as it turns out, was a central figure in rewriting the Court's doctrine on intervention. Sopinka had thought about interest group intervention as a practicing lawyer. Shortly before he was appointed to the Court, in May 1987, and just as the Court was beginning to respond to the criticisms that the interest groups and legal commentators had made, he delivered a public speech on interest group intervention (Sopinka 1988). The speech showed that he was familiar with all the commentary and interest group lobbying the issue had generated, and agreed that the Supreme Court's approach to intervention was too narrow. It was not, he thought, in keeping with the Court's new role in the Charter era. He advocated a more lenient approach to intervention and advanced two specific recommendations for the Court. First, he recommended that once the Court decides to hear a particular case, it should "expand the scope of participation so that all legitimate interests are fully represented" in the case. This might not happen, he warned, "if the two parties are left to their own devices" (884). Secondly, he recommended that the Court also allow interveners to widen the scope of cases. The Court was sticking too closely to the adjudicative model by "declining to open the strict confines of the *lis inter partes*" and not acknowledging that it needed "a wide variety of inputs to decide quasi-political questions" (884). Sopinka specifically cited Bryden's 1987 paper and the public concerns raised by the Canadian Bar Association, the CCLA and the Canadian Labour Congress.

By the time Sopinka was appointed to the bench, the Supreme Court had already started to accept interveners more frequently. However, it had not yet elaborated on its 1987 rules on intervention. Since Sopinka had clearly reflected on the issue before he joined the Court, and was familiar with both the legal commentary and the interest group positions on the issue, he was well placed to flesh out the Court's new rules. He soon had an opportunity to do so. In 1988, Suzanne Côté applied to intervene in the *Reference re: Newfoundland Workers' Compensation Act*. Sopinka was assigned to hear her application. The reference case asked the Court to decide whether provincial workers' compensation schemes that forced the victims of workplace accidents to accept statutory compensation for their injuries violated the Charter. Côté was only interested in the reference because she had a similar case pending against the British Columbia government. Given the peculiar facts of the reference, Sopinka could have let Côté intervene without rewriting the Court's rules. The reference grew out of an earlier case that challenged Newfoundland's workers' compensation legislation. A widow had challenged the legislation in the Newfoundland Supreme Court. Her husband had died while on the job and she claimed that the Charter's section 15 equality rights guaranteed her a right to sue for compensation. The trial judge rejected her case because her husband had died before the Charter's equality rights had come into force, but hinted that the act did violate the Charter nonetheless. These comments immediately cast doubts on the Newfoundland workers' compensation system and the government moved quickly to clarify the situation with a reference case. By the time the reference got to the Supreme Court, it had attracted several interveners. The widow who originally challenged the act intervened to oppose it at the Supreme Court of Canada, but her interest in the issue was strictly moot. The other interveners in the reference all supported the act. Therefore, without Côté's intervention, the reference would have been unbalanced, and devoid of a concrete adjudicative context. So, Sopinka could have allowed Côté to intervene simply to give the reference some adjudicative context, and left matters at that.

Instead, he decided go farther. He issued written reasons to justify his decision to let Côté intervene. These reasons were the Court's first comprehensive interpretation of its 1987 rules on intervention, and they in effect rewrote the rules. The 1987 rules had set out two criteria for judging the merits of an application to intervene. First, the would-be intervener had to demonstrate it had an interest in the case in question. Secondly, it had to show that its position in the case would be different from the positions of the parties and be useful to the Court. Sopinka began his reasons by reinterpreting the "interest" prong of the rule. *Any* interest, he wrote, would be sufficient to meet this prong of the test, and he declined to place any restrictions on what kind of "interest" a would-be intervener would have to demonstrate.[5] Even having a similar case pending at a lower level of the court system could establish a "tenuous" interest. Effectively, Sopinka's reasons eliminated the "interest" prong of the intervention test altogether. If a group has enough interest in a case to apply for leave to intervene, it has enough interest to meet Sopinka's new interpretation of the "interest" prong. Sopinka then turned to the "useful and different submissions" prong of the 1987 rule. Groups and individuals could "easily" satisfy this prong of the test if they had "a history of involvement in the issue giving the applicant an expertise which can shed fresh light or provide new information on the matter." He then noted, "It is more difficult for a private litigant to demonstrate that his or her argument will be different" (340). This line of reasoning turned the "useful and different submissions" prong into a test of the applicant's reputation and track record. This new interpretation effectively gave "repeat players" an advantage in getting leave to intervene. Sopinka's reasons in the *Côté* application implemented the first recommendation he had made in his 1987 speech by allowing any group the Court deemed to have a "legitimate" interest in a case to intervene.

In two applications he heard during 1991, Sopinka had an opportunity to implement the second part of his 1988 speech—

letting interveners widen the scope of the *lis* in a case. Until 1991, the Supreme Court had forbidden interveners from adding new legal issues to a case. Even a court that sees a case primarily as an opportunity to make new law should have some regard for the original parties to a case and not make them argue additional issues in their appeal. Using a case as a pretext for making new law is one thing, but letting interveners add new legal issues to an existing dispute would be unfair to the parties that launched the case. In 1991, Sopinka heard LEAF's application to intervene in the *M(K) v M(H)* (1992) and *Norberg* (1992) cases. Both cases involved private rather than public law issues and in both cases the parties had been content to argue them as private law cases. LEAF applied to intervene in these cases in order to raise Charter arguments. This would have turned two private law disputes into public, Charter cases, yet Sopinka gave LEAF leave to intervene. His written reasons for doing so left the door open for LEAF to raise Charter issues in the cases. Not even the commentators who had urged the Court to loosen its approach to intervention had pushed the Court to go this far. Letting an intervener make its own arguments on the legal points already at issue in an appeal takes a court away from a strict focus on adjudication, but it does so only to broaden the range of arguments on those points before the Court. Letting an intervener raise legal issues that are not already part of an appeal means the Court has abandoned any pretense of settling the original legal dispute altogether. Sopinka's reasons in *M(K)* and *Norberg* implemented the second part of his 1987 recommendations, and took the Court beyond even what the commentators had proposed in the law reviews.

Sopinka's reasoning in the *Côté*, *M(K)*, and *Norberg* rewrote the Supreme Court's doctrine on intervention and went beyond the demands of the legal commentators. Any organization that the Court recognized as having a legitimate and ongoing involvement in an issue would be heard. Once an organization had established a track record, it would be allowed to intervene whenever it wished. Moreover, favored interveners would be allowed to use a Supreme Court case to raise constitutional issues not raised in the case. By 1991, he had made good on the ideas on interest group intervention he had set out before he joined the Court.

## The Problem of Differential Treatment

Sopinka never set out a test for determining which would-be interveners have enough of a "history of involvement" in an issue to give it "an expertise which can shed fresh light or provide new information" to the Court. This part of his reasons in *Côté* echoed his 1988 comment that all "legitimate" interests should be heard at the Supreme Court. Despite Sopinka's optimistic words and the Court's record of accepting most applications for leave to intervene, the Court has not treated all groups alike. Some get a chillier reception than others do.

In the wake of Sopinka's reasoning in the *Côté* application, other judges made decisions about interveners that are hard to square with the Sopinka's trilogy of intervention applications. In January 1991, L'Heureux-Dubé heard applications from would-be interveners in the *Zundel* appeal (1992). Zundel had been convicted of "spreading false news" by denying certain aspects of the Holocaust, and Zundel claimed the Criminal Code's false news provision violated his right to freedom of expression. L'Heureux-Dubé let the CCLA, the Canadian Jewish Congress, and the League for Human Rights of the B'Nai Brith intervene in the case, but refused leave to Simon Weisenthal or the Canadian Holocaust Remembrance Association. The two unsuccessful applicants were as interested in the issue of hate propaganda as the three that were successful, and both had long histories of involvement in the issue. Yet, L'Heureux-Dubé gave no reason why the first two groups should be heard and not the other two. Why were they turned away? Two years later, in March 1993, McLachlin heard applications from would-be interveners in the *Finta* case. Finta had been convicted of committing war crimes during World War II under Canada's then-new war crimes legislation. His appeal raised a number of complex Charter challenges to the legislation. McLachlin allowed the Canadian Jewish Congress, the League for Human Rights of the B'Nai Brith, and InterAmicus to intervene, but rejected an application from Kenneth Narvey. McLachlin recognized that "Mr. Narvey is a qualified expert in the subject matter before this Court," but she turned him away because "his interest in the outcome of the litigation cannot be established merely by his status as a researcher and advocate on public law issues" (Finta 1993, 1143). Yet, after Sopinka's decision on the *Côté* application, any *interest group* can satisfy the first prong of the test merely by virtue of applying to intervene. Was Narvey turned away simply because he was an individual and not a group? Finally, in the 1993 *Morgentaler* case, the Court heard a constitutional challenge to Nova Scotia's medical service legislation that prohibited abortions from being performed outside of hospitals. Sopinka himself stopped the Canadian Abortion Rights Action League from adding a new ground to the list of constitutional challenges already raised in the case. He had previously allowed LEAF to turn *M(K)* and *Norberg* into Charter cases. Why not let CARAL raise a new constitutional issue where one party had already made a constitutional challenge? Did he think of LEAF as a more "legitimate" group than CARAL?

The Court's most jarring decision regarding interveners came in the *Lavigne* appeal. Lavigne challenged the Ontario labor law that forces all employees in a certified bargaining unit to pay dues to the union representing that bargaining unit regardless of whether an employee belongs to the union. This test case, sponsored by the National Citizens Coalition, claimed the law violated Lavigne's Charter right to freedom of association. In this instance, the Court used the intervener mechanism to punish the National Citizens' Coalition for pursuing the case at all. Four trade union federations intervened to defend the law, and the Court forced Lavigne, and by extension the NCC, to pay their costs in the case (*Lavigne* 1991). Until this point, the Court had adhered to the rule that "no costs are awarded to or against any intervenant" (*Harper* 1980, 16). Legal commentators had unanimously repeated the Court's point. It was a settled point "that a friend of the court cannot benefit from a cost award" (Scriven and Muldoon 1985, 472). "Public interest intervenors should be responsible for their own costs regardless of the outcome of the litigation" (Bryden 1987, 523). They "should not expect to be rewarded if they succeed or penalized if they fail" (523, fn. 113).[6] Yet, the Supreme Court breached this rule in *Lavigne*. It imposed the interveners' costs on the NCC.[7] The National Citizens' Coalition is a high profile, conservative interest group whose slogan is "more freedom through less government."[8] LEAF and the NCC come from opposite ends of the political spectrum. Based on the Court's track record, it is hard to avoid concluding that the Court will let LEAF push the envelope on intervention but penalize the NCC for challenging the power of Canada's trade unions. Aside from Crane and Brown's description of *Lavigne* as "unusual" (1995, 170), the law reviews have not seen a single criticism of the case from the commentators on intervention.

Sopinka's intervention trilogy was supposed to establish that any legitimate interest group with a history of involvement in an issue, and the ability to shed new light on the issue for the Court, would get leave to intervene. Yet, the Court seems to have had difficulty applying that rule. Why hear from the Canadian Jewish Congress and League for Human Rights, but not from Simon Wisenthal or the Canadian Holocaust Remembrance League? Sopinka had decided that interveners would be allowed to widen the scope of the legal dispute in a case. Yet, he allowed LEAF to turn private law cases into public law cases, but did not allow CARAL to widen the scope of the 1993 *Morgentaler* appeal. Moreover, the NCC certainly was entitled to see the Court's decision in *Lavigne* as a sharp signal that it should not be challenging unions. It is hard to escape the conclusion that the Court plays favorites with interest groups. Favored groups can intervene when they wish and bend cases to raise the issues they want raised. Other groups have difficulty getting in the door.

## Law, Politics, and Intervention

These problems in dealing with interveners point to a deeper conundrum for the Supreme Court. By taking a lenient approach to interveners, the Court has implicitly rejected the legalistic version of judicial supremacy and opted for the political version of judicial supremacy. Yet, the Court, like the commentators who urged it to adopt a political view of its role, is unwilling to accept all the implications of conceding that judicial review is a political exercise. If judicial review is a political exercise, why must courts have the final say in the interpretation of the constitution? Why, in a democratic regime, must their interpretation of constitutional law trump those of other political institutions? Bryden's argument provides the bluntest statement of this conundrum. While he argues that judicial review is a political function and judges make law when they engage in constitutional judicial review, he also wants to limit the recourse for those who are dissatisfied with judge-made constitutional law. "The whole point of a constitutionally entrenched charter of rights is that there are principles that we regard as so fundamental that we want to place restraints on our ability collectively to interfere with them" (1987, 510). The "political branches" cannot be allowed to undo the work of the judiciary.

Here Bryden is caught in what appears to be a contradiction. He bases his argument for interest group intervention on a political view of judicial review, but he reverts to the legalistic argument to isolate judicial review from the "political branches" of government. He tries to reconcile these two points by appealing to Dworkin's familiar legalistic argument that the judiciary is the forum of principled decision making and the other institutions of government are where interest-driven decision making prevails. According to Bryden, an inherent part of the Charter project was "a belief that it is possible to discuss these [divisive social] issues and find principled ways to resolve them" (1987, 510). The judiciary works out these issues in a principled way. "If the courts are to succeed in playing the difficult role . . . they will have to be sensitive to the interests and points of view of all who are likely to be affected by their decisions . . . " and accept interest group intervention (511). Such a sensitivity will assuage concerns "about the courts' lack of political accountability" (511). When Bryden relies on Dworkin's distinction between the realms of law and politics to justify intervention, he further undermines his claim that judicial review is essentially political. This makes his apparent contradiction worse. On the one hand, he advances the legalistic justification for judicial review. The Charter puts some issues outside of politics and into the realm of law. On the other hand, he rejects the legalistic argument for judicial review. Judges, like any other politicians, should be sensitive to the political interests that are involved in any particular issue. They should hear from interest group interveners when they decide Charter cases. These two points cannot be easily reconciled. He claims that judicial review is inherently political, but also wants to put judicial review beyond the reach of politics.

The Supreme Court is now caught in the same conundrum. It accepts the political nature of judicial review when dealing with interest groups. It thinks it must be sensitive to the concerns of groups that will be affected by its decisions, and gives them a role that goes far beyond what would be required if judicial review were purely legalistic. Yet, when faced with the prospect of a challenge to its claim of judicial supremacy it responds with a legalistic justification of judicial review. When the Court ordered Alberta to extend the protection of its human rights code to homosexuals in the 1998 case of *Vriend*, it knew the decision would provoke a backlash in that province. The issue of whether the province's human rights law ought to forbid discrimination based on sexual orientation had been debated again and again and both the government and the legislature had decided not to do so. In *Vriend*, the Court was deliberately challenging these judgments. It knew its decision would provoke harsh criticism in Alberta. It anticipated its critics by canvassing the debates on the legitimacy of judicial review. It then responded by reiterating the legalistic argument for judicial review:

> Because the courts are independent from the executive and legislature, litigants and citizens generally can rely on the courts to make reasoned and principled decisions according to the dictates of the constitution even though specific decisions may not be universally acclaimed. In carrying out their duties, courts are not to second-guess legislatures and the executives; they are not to make value judgments on what they regard as the proper policy choice; this is for the other branches. Rather, the courts are to uphold the Constitution and have been expressly invited to perform that role by the Constitution itself. But respect by the courts for the legislature and executive role is as important as ensuring that the other branches respect each other's role and the role of the courts. (1998, 564–565)

If the Court's role in *Vriend* was purely legalistic, why did it let fourteen interest groups intervene in the case? If the Court was merely upholding the Constitution and not making a value judgement, why did it feel it needed the help of the Alberta Civil Liberties Association, LEAF, the Canadian Jewish Congress, and Focus on the Family? The Court is trying to have it both ways—having all the fun of making political decisions under the guise of interpreting constitutional law, but offering up a legalistic defense of its work whenever its activism is questioned.

## CONCLUSION

When challenged, the Supreme Court continues to rely on a legalistic justification for judicial review, but, by 1991, the political implications of its approach to interest group intervention had become clear. The Court's decision to take on a new role in the Canadian constitutional order was encouraged and legitimated by an advocacy campaign on the part of legal commentators writing in law journals. These commentators also gave the Court a way to legitimate its new political role, by bringing disadvantaged groups into its work. While the Court has increased the number of interest group interveners in its work, it has applied different rules for different kinds of groups. Some preferred groups can push the boundaries of intervention, by expanding the scope of court cases and imposing new burdens on the parties to those cases.

How do groups benefit from this alliance with the Court? What is so valuable about being a preferred interest group at the Supreme Court? What kind of status can the Supreme Court confer on a group, and how is that status valuable? Status is an odd commodity. The next chapter turns to these questions.

# 4

## THE MARKET FOR
## SECTION 15 STATUS

O f all the Charter's provisions, the section 15 equality rights
guarantees provide the widest scope for interest group litigation. Interest group activists lobbied ferociously over the wording of section 15 when it was being drafted. The Supreme Court
of Canada has turned the section into a proscriptive program to
achieve equality of results among selected groups in Canadian
society. It has read a heavy dose of the political disadvantage theory
into section 15. Groups that the Court considers "disadvantaged"
can use the Charter's equality rights to fend off government
policies that impose burdens on them, or to claim access to
policies that might advance their interests. Status as a disadvantaged group is therefore a valuable resource, and groups now
compete for that status.

Status is recognition in a hierarchy that lets those who hold
it stake preferential claims on the political resources of the state
or preferential access to the political process itself. Status is an
odd commodity, though. This chapter uses a rational choice
modeling technique, Schelling Curves, to demonstrate how the
dynamics of status seeking influences group choices about whether

to engage in equality rights litigation. The model developed here provides predictions about how interest groups approach an open-ended grant of status such as section 15. Most importantly, the model shows that the politics of status has intrinsic limits. Once section 15 aimed to equalize group outcomes in Canadian society, it was no longer about equality, but about constitutionalizing a hierarchy of groups. The Canadian state cannot pursue equality for all groups at once—that would lead back to the equality-of-individuals approach that the groups that lobbied over section 15 wanted to avoid. The Supreme Court must choose which groups it will recognize with the status of historically disadvantaged group. Not every group can get into that "club." The model elaborated here concludes that the politics of status is driven by the incentives that status seeking poses for interest groups.

Legal status is perhaps the most highly institutionalized form of status (Clark 1995, 17), and the Canadian Constitution has long been used to confer legal status on social groups (Knopff and Morton 1992, chapter 4). In 1867, English-speaking as well as Protestant minorities in Quebec, and Roman Catholic minorities in Ontario were given special rights over language and education. The 1982 constitutional amendments conferred new forms of status on new groups. The constitutional amendments that Prime Minister Mulroney and the provincial premiers proposed in the 1987 Meech Lake Accord would have given the province of Quebec special status as a "distinct society" within Canada. Those amendments failed in part because the groups that received constitutional status in 1982 saw the distinct society provisions in the Meech Lake Accord as threatening to their new status (Cairns 1988). In 1992, the prime minister and the premiers revisited the question of constitutional status in the Charlottetown Accord. They proposed adding a "Canada Clause" to the Constitution to set out the relative status of Quebec, women, English and French minorities, native Canadians, and many other groups. Group competition for status is now a central feature, perhaps the central feature, of Canadian constitutional politics. Groups fight battles over constitutional status with tremendous sophistication.

SECTION 15: EQUALITY RIGHTS IN THE
CANADIAN CONSTITUTION

Section 15 of the Charter has attracted a great deal of interest
from would-be interest group litigators. This is no surprise. As
noted in chapter 2, many interest groups saw the constitutional
reform process of the early 1980s as an opportunity to expand the
possibilities for "public interest litigation" in Canada. The
centrepiece of the Trudeau government's original package of constitutional reforms was the proposed Canadian Charter of Rights
and Freedoms, which included a section on "nondiscrimination
rights" that prohibited government discrimination on a variety of
grounds.[1] These groups quickly realized that the nondiscrimination rights could provide a wide scope for interest group litigation
if they were properly drafted. They set about lobbying for the
most favorable possible wording of what would become section
15 of the Charter. The courts had taken a restrained approach to
the interpretation of the nondiscrimination rights in the 1960
Canadian Bill of Rights, only once invalidating a federal statute for
violating the Bill's nondiscrimination clause (Manfredi 1993a, 128–
132). These groups wanted the courts to give the Charter a more
activist reading. To give the courts the room to do so, they wanted
the Charter's nondiscrimination rights relabeled as "equality rights,"
and they wanted the equality rights expanded to establish new
rights that would carry the force of constitutional law. These groups
lobbied to change the equality-of-opportunity emphasis of the
nondiscrimination rights to a group-based equality-of-result emphasis. Shifting the emphasis to an equality-of-group-results approach inherently granted constitutional status to groups. The
state can only pursue equality for a few groups without reverting
to the equality-of-individuals approach that these groups rejected.[2]

When the federal government eventually redrafted section 15
along these lines, not surprisingly, groups began to compete for
this status. Speaking of the patriation exercise generally, Knopff
and Morton write that

> a variety of groups, especially women and aboriginals,
> perceived the opportunity to enhance their own status

and to acquire valuable legal resources by having their identities explicitly enshrined in Charter provisions. They thus lobbied hard to secure the most favourable Charter wording possible. (1992, 81)

While feminist groups lobbied the Trudeau government to ensure that section 15 would allow judges to review a full range of government programs for their equality impact, other groups representing disabled and homosexual Canadians wanted section 15 status extended to them. In the end, the government decided to outlaw discrimination based on a few grounds in the text of section 15, and to allow judges to add to the list of protected groups. The text of the Charter lists a number of grounds upon which discrimination is expressly prohibited ("race, national or ethnic origin, colour, religion, sex, age or mental or physical disability") and these "enumerated" grounds provide some guide to identifying the groups that the Charter's equality rights protect. The enumerated grounds of discrimination, however, are not intended to be an exhaustive list; they are only "particular" prohibited grounds of discrimination. Other groups can ask the courts to create "unenumerated" grounds of prohibited discrimination and thus gain protected status from judges. In effect, the drafters of the Charter delegated to the courts the task of determining who, in addition to the enumerated groups, would get section 15 protection and what criteria would be used in extending this status. They moved the competition for section 15 status out of the constitutional amendment process and into the courts.

Once the Charter was finalized, the groups faced two problems. If the courts restrained themselves in using the Charter, the value of section 15 status would be lost. The judiciary's reluctance to strike down legislation using the nondiscrimination clause of the 1960 Bill of Rights left doubts in many minds about the courts' willingness to use their powers actively. Just as importantly, if judges read too many new grounds into section 15's open-ended wording, they would extend status to so many groups that it would lose their value to any one group. Nothing in the Charter's text limits how far the courts can go in granting section 15 status. If judges decided to use their Charter powers actively, but spread section 15 status too widely, the original status groups would hardly be farther ahead.

In the end, the Supreme Court of Canada did not disappoint the original section 15 groups. In its key section 15 cases, *Andrews* (1989) and *Turpin* (1989), it laid out an active approach to using the section. It advertised that it would make more active use of section 15 than it had made of the Bill of Rights. Just as importantly, it decided to use the political disadvantage theory to limit the number of groups it would protect using section 15. Groups covered by the grounds of discrimination set out in the text of the section would be able to ask for the courts' protection. Other groups that are "discrete and insular minorities," or that have historically suffered social disadvantage, would also be able to get the protection of the courts under section 15 (Manfredi 1993a, 142–152). In making decisions about which groups would get such protection, the Court, in Wilson's words, should not just look to "the context of the law which is subject to challenge" but also to "the place of the group in the entire social, political and legal fabric of our society."[3] "While legislatures must inevitably draw distinctions among the governed, such distinctions should not bring about or reinforce the disadvantage of certain groups and individuals by denying them the rights freely accorded to others" (*Andrews* 1989, 152).

This test closes section 15's open-endedness and ensures that not all groups will be able to gain protected status. As LEAF activist Lynn Smith has noted, the Supreme Court has "constricted the entrance into the equality rights section" to those in disadvantaged groups (1994, 62). Thus, the Supreme Court has created a two-stage process for groups that want to exploit section 15 in court. First, they must gain status as a "protected group" for the purposes of section 15 by proving their disadvantage. Then, through the courts, they may seek protection from government policies that harm them or ask for the extension of government programs that would help them. Constricting entry to section 15 allows the courts to bring unintended discrimination into the application of equality rights. It also allows the courts to let the government treat disadvantaged groups differently from other groups (Smith 1994, 63).

This "asymmetrical approach" to equality rights (Smith 1994, 63) let the Supreme Court make a decision such as *Weatherall* (1993). In that case, a group of men serving time in a federal prison complained that while prison regulations stopped male guards from conducting certain kinds of searches of female prisoners, female guards were allowed to conduct such searches of male prisoners. The Court ruled that the regulations do not violate a prisoner's equality rights. Historically, men perpetrate violence against women but few women perpetrate violence against men. Moreover, women are socially disadvantaged compared to men. Thus, cross-gender frisks are more threatening to women prisoners than to men. Section 15 protects women because they are a historically disadvantaged group, but offers no protection to men.

Since 1985, the courts have been asked to add many unenumerated grounds of discrimination to those set out in section 15, and therefore to extend "protected" status to new groups. The Supreme Court of Canada named citizenship as an unenumerated ground of prohibited discrimination in its first section 15 case,[4] effectively extending equality rights protection to immigrants. More recently, the courts have adopted the federal government's reasoning that sexual orientation is an unenumerated ground of discrimination. Homosexuals are a protected group.[5] In litigation in Prince Edward Island, two accountants asked the courts to declare that Certified General Accountants are protected by section 15 from governmental discrimination in allocating the power to conduct public audits among professional associations of accountants.[6]

Given that judges will be hard-pressed to give "protected" status to a new group unless the group asks for it, the list of section 15 status groups will be shaped more by the incentives facing interest groups than by principles of constitutional jurisprudence. Therefore, it is important to look at the conditions under which a group has an incentive to seek that status. Will judges always be faced with demands from groups that they be given equality rights protection? If not, then the criteria judges set for granting equality rights status will not shape section 15's impact as much as the incentives for interest groups. So, under what conditions will a potentially protected group have an incentive to seek equality rights status under section 15 and under what conditions will it not have such an incentive? The incentives facing interest groups ought to set the bounds for the politics of constitutional equality rights status in Canada and also provide generalizable lessons about the politics of status seeking in other situations.

Knopff and Morton (1992) provide the only systematic treatment of how the "politics of status" work in the courtroom. "Constitutional status gives a group official public status of the highest order, and groups who enjoy it have an advantage in pressing their claims against government over other groups who do not" (82). They point out, though, that status is not a limitless commodity. "Although virtually all significant political entities have come to see constitutional status as a good thing, its value is diluted the more widely it is dispersed. . . . If too many rivals enjoy an equal constitutional status, this advantage disappears" (82). This property of status is well known in the broader literature on status. "If a hundred Nobel Peace Prizes were awarded annually, each prize would be much less prestigious" (Milner 1994, 34). As will also become apparent below, status can lose its value if it is too narrowly allocated.

The question of who will seek section 15 status involves issues of competing incentives for individual political decision makers. Rational choice theory provides a useful perspective for elaborating the dynamics of status seeking. The decision of whether or not to seek section 15 status is a binary one for an interest group (either it tries to get such status or it does not) and it creates externalities (the choices of the other groups influence the incentives that govern any single group's choice). Thomas Schelling has developed a simple set of curves for representing such decisions. These curves can model the incentives that apply to a status-seeking situation. A Schelling Curve of Section 15 Status would formalize Knopff and Morton's observations, provide additional insights into the dynamics of the politics of status, and supply concrete predictions about the behavior of potentially protected groups and those groups that already enjoy section 15 status. It could also be extended to produce a general theory of status-seeking politics.

### SCHELLING CURVES

In his Fels Lectures, Schelling (1978) develops a graphic method for depicting the incentives that face many decision makers when they must make a binary decision involving externalities. These

"Schelling Curves" also assume that the order in which each individual arrives at the chance to make the decision makes no difference to the situation. A Schelling Curve is a useful, nontechnical way to model certain types of decision-making situations.

A Schelling Curve models the decisions of n + 1 individuals in a given situation, a single individual to be studied and n others. Each individual incurs a cost (C) for switching from one choice to the other, and receives a benefit $(V_i)$. Thus, the net benefit for switching choices is $V_i$ C. Schelling originally designed these curves to model multiple-player prisoner's dilemma situations. Recall the classic prisoner's dilemma with two prisoners (see Figure 4.1).[7] The police arrest two guilty burglars and lock them in different cells. Each prisoner knows that if he confesses to the crime while his partner keeps quiet, he can cut a deal with the prosecutor to get a short sentence. His partner will receive a very long prison term. They also know that if they both keep quiet they will get medium-length sentences for possessing housebreaking tools. Finally, if both confess, they will both get long sentences. The usual depiction of this situation, shown in Figure 4.1, demonstrates that

**Prisoner 2**

|  |  | Confess | Keep Quiet |
|---|---|:---:|:---:|
|  | **Confess** | −1, −1 | 5,0 |
| **Prisoner 1** | | | |
|  | **Keep Quiet** | 0,5 | 3,3 |

*Notes:*
The numbers show payoffs,, or net benefits, to the prisoners in ordinal numbers. The payoffs to Prisoner 1 (the row player) are shown first and the payoffs to Prisoner 2 (the column player) second

**Figure 4.1** The Prisoner's Dilemma for Two Decision Makers.

both prisoners have an incentive to confess in the hope of getting a reduced sentence. Of course, if both confess, they will both end up in prison. Collectively, then, they would be better off if they both keep quiet; however, neither can take the chance that his partner will confess and send him to prison for a long sentence. Their independent, rational decisions produce a collectively inferior result.

If there are many individuals making decisions in this situation, the incentives can be modeled as shown in Figure 4.2. This is the simplest Schelling Curve. The vertical axis measures the net benefit to the individual for choosing one or the other of the options. The horizontal axis shows the number of individuals keeping quiet instead of confessing. Every individual's dominant strategy is always to confess, although the benefit he receives by confessing depends on the number of other prisoners that are keeping quiet. The only equilibrium in this situation is for all players to confess.[8] If enough prisoners could be convinced to keep quiet, eventually their benefits from keeping quiet would exceed their benefits if everyone confessed. At this point, known

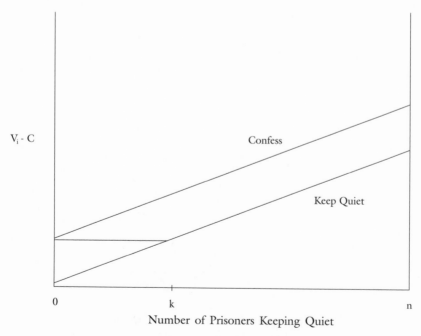

**Figure 4.2** The Multiple-Player Prisoner's Dilemma Schelling Curve.

as the k-point, each prisoner would still be better off by confessing than by keeping quiet. Therefore, in the prisoner's dilemma a k-group probably will not emerge. Still, a coalition might emerge such that its members will be better off than they would if they and everyone else chose to pursue the superior strategy.

A variation on this simple Schelling Curve models the situation facing individual codfishing boats off the Newfoundland coast (see Figure 4.3). The federal Department of Fisheries and Oceans sets quotas for each boat in an effort to preserve the North Atlantic cod stocks. The ideal situation for any single boat captain is to bust his quota by fishing for cod at will while all other boats

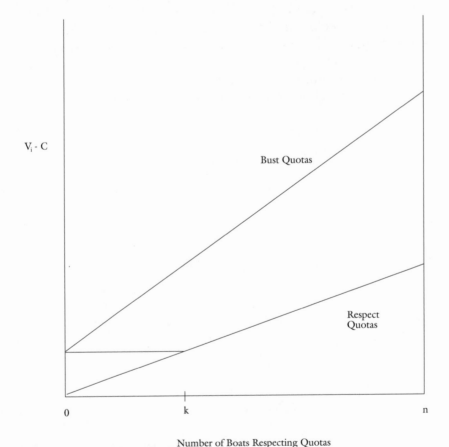

**Figure 4.3** Schelling Curve of Cod Quotas.

respect their quotas. In such a situation, other boats will limit their harvests of fish to preserve the North Atlantic cod stocks, while the single boat will be able to reap enormous harvests of fish. Of course, the same incentives face all boat captains and therefore they should all fish at will, busting their quotas, and driving the North Atlantic cod into oblivion. This situation differs from the one in the simplest Schelling Curve depicted in Figure 4.2. As more and more boats respect their quotas, it becomes more attractive for a single boat to bust its quota, since the conservation efforts of the other boats will mean there are more cod to fish.[9]

The Schelling Curve technique can be applied to situations where there is no single choice that is always to the advantage of every player. For example, Schelling himself speaks of a vaccination curve. This is shown in Figure 4.4. Vaccination protects an individual against contracting some horrible disease from others. There is a small chance of contracting the disease from the vaccine itself. If few of the people around you have been vaccinated for a disease, you have an incentive to get vaccinated in order to protect yourself. But if all the people around you have been vaccinated, you run a greater risk of contracting the disease from the vaccine than from the people around you and you might chose to forego vaccination. As more of the population get vaccinated, the incentive to remain unvaccinated increases. When enough other people around you get vaccinated, you have no incentive to get vaccinated. The curves cross. At this "v-point,"[10] the incentives change for an individual decision maker.

## A SCHELLING CURVE OF EQUALITY RIGHTS STATUS

In constructing a Schelling Curve of Equality Rights Status, all the groups that could potentially gain protected status are the $n + 1$ individual decision makers. The universe of potentially protected groups is large. The original text of section 15 protects many groups, and groups representing gays, lesbians, prisoners, the poor, ethnocultural groups, and the "environmentally sensitive" have mounted judicial campaigns to secure "protected" status for their constituents.[11] If the courts had given accountants section 15

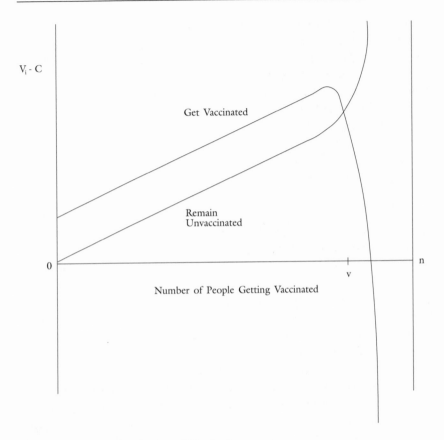

$V_i$ - C

Get Vaccinated

Remain
Unvaccinated

0

v

n

Number of People Getting Vaccinated

**Figure 4.4** Schelling Curve of Vaccination.

protection in PEI, other professional and economic interests would be staking equality rights claims as well.[12]

Each potentially protected group has two options. It can either try to get protected status from judges, or it can opt not to participate in status-seeking politics under section 15. Becoming a protected group entails certain costs. A group might incur considerable legal fees in pursuing a claim. More dauntingly, it must get some support for its claim in academic and legal circles before it goes to court. A group's claim gets a basic legitimacy from support in law journals and other legal publications.[13] A group benefits from protected status because it bolsters that group's claims in the wider policy-making process. For example, equality rights considerations have led policy makers to extend existing social programs and legal protections to status groups, and to begin redesigning Canada's tax code to alleviate its burden on status groups (Monahan and Finkelstein 1993).[14] Groups that opt out of equality rights politics get none of these benefits. They do bear the cost both of adjudicating status claims launched by other groups and of supplying the government benefits conferred on status groups.

The basic Schelling Curve of Equality Rights Status is shown in Figure 4.5. Groups that opt out of equality rights politics suffer a slight disadvantage compared to other groups. They must bear the cost of adjudicating the cases launched by other groups and of government compliance with the decisions in those cases. Whether a given group should seek status depends on how many other groups already share it. A group does not always have an interest in seeking protected status. At the left end of the curve, where too few other groups have protection, the status is too esoteric to be of any good. It is too "avant-garde" to attract the

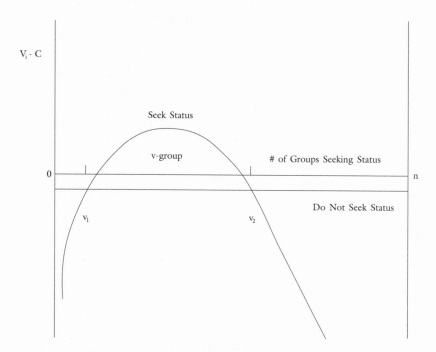

**Figure 4.5** Schelling Curve of Section 15 Status.

attention of judges, the legal profession and of other potentially protected groups, just as a fashion trend in clothing that is followed by too few people might be too "avant-garde" to be truly fashionable. Feminist groups worried that the final 1981 draft of section 15 extended equality rights status to too many groups and that this status had been diluted too far (Knopff and Morton 1992, 87–88). They wanted sex discrimination to be connected with discrimination based on other highly suspect grounds such as race and religion rather than less suspect grounds such as age and disability. Yet, the curve in Figure 4.5 suggests that if only a few interests had been advanced by section 15, then equality rights status might well have been too obscure to attract attention from Canadian judges and the legal profession. Would section 15 status have taken hold if it had been given to fewer groups? Based on the empirical record, it is hard to say, but extending equality rights status to racial and ethnic groups seems to have expanded the list of protected groups far enough to make such status less exotic and thus more acceptable. Moreover, if fewer groups had been included in section 15 in 1980 and 1981, it might have been harder for the groups that were included to form a minimum winning coalition on such issues as trying to get the federal treasury to help pay for their litigation through programs such as the Court Challenges Program. Undoubtedly it would have been more difficult to get the Court Challenges Program established or resurrected if only a few interests had been recognized in section 15. With the bargaining power of ethnic groups, disabled groups and so on, the Court Challenges Program coalition had a better chance of success.[15]

Once the v-group forms, other groups find it advantageous to seek equality rights status; in fact, becoming a protected group is the superior choice for potentially protected groups once the $v_1$ point is passed. When a v-group forms, additional potentially protected groups should soon rush into court to press their cases for being granted equality rights status. This process is now underway in Canadian courtrooms as homosexual groups, prisoners' groups, poverty groups, ethnic groups, groups for the "environmentally sensitive," and professional accountants' associations advance their claims to protected status.

Finally, at the right end of the curve, so many groups have attained equality rights status that this status is no longer valuable.

Too many groups begin pressing for the limited number of spots on the Supreme Court's docket. Too many groups become eligible for federal subsidies through programs such as the Court Challenges Program (see chapter 5). This is the situation that Knopff and Morton identify when they speak of the value of status disappearing. Just as the fashion value of a clothing label declines when too many people wear it, so status as a protected group is only valuable if the family of protected groups is an elite among groups. Once too many groups attain section 15 status, it becomes worthless. When the political process hands out status, there are maximum as well as minimum winning coalitions (Riker 1962).

If the curve in Figure 4.5 is correct, at some point existing protected groups either have to protect the currency of their status by opposing the campaigns of other groups to become protected, or they have to seek newer and higher forms of status in constitutional law. To date, existing protected groups have not intervened in court cases to oppose the extension of protected status to other groups. LEAF, for example, did not actively oppose the extension of equality rights status to homosexuals. Yet, LEAF has always been cool to the idea of expanding the family of status groups through judicial interpretation (Hausegger 1994), and the feminists who later created LEAF tried to keep age and disability out of section 15's text during the drafting of the Charter (Knopff 1989, 43). In the Supreme Court of Canada's first section 15 case, LEAF was among the groups arguing that equality rights status ought to be limited to groups, such as women, who were the victims of historical disadvantage in Canadian society. In effect, it tried to limit the size of the v-group by urging the Supreme Court of Canada to use rather narrow criteria in expanding it. In the future, we may see organizations representing existing protected groups opposing the attempts of other groups to get equality rights status.[16]

## THE QUESTION OF COSTS

The diagram in Figure 4.5 assumes that the cost of becoming a protected group is constant for all potentially protected groups. There are three possible objections to this assumption. First, one objection is that as judges get used to the idea of equality rights status, the difficulty of convincing them to extend such status might decline. Secondly, a related objection is that judges might be biased toward the claims of certain types of groups over those of other types of groups. Finally, government programs that subsidize interest group litigation such as the Court Challenges Program might change the costs associated with advancing a claim to equality rights protection.

The first objection, that the cost of becoming a protected group drops as more and more groups become protected, is plausible and without empirical data it is impossible to deny that such an effect exists. Such a decline in the costs of becoming a protected group, however, simply enlarges the v-group by moving the $v_2$ point farther to the right in Figure 4.5. In effect, such a variation in the assumptions underlying the diagram merely postpones the point at which it is no longer in a group's interest to seek section 15 status. It does not change the prediction that eventually groups will no longer gain a net benefit through section 15 status.

The second objection, that judges might be biased in favor of the claims of some groups over those of others, does not change the shape of the curve in Figure 4.5. Judicial bias simply reduces the costs of seeking status for certain groups and therefore allows a prediction about exactly which groups will form the v-group. If judges are biased toward some groups and make this apparent, a v-group will still form but it will not be formed from a random selection of interest groups. Instead, it will likely fill up with interest groups that enjoy the affections of judges.

Finally, while the Court Challenges Program does reduce the cost of gaining status for groups that it funds, not all groups are able to get its funding. Existing status groups have used the program to protect their status. The program has not funded groups that its officials think violate their idea of equality rights in Canada. It has acted as a filter (see chapter 5). Since the existing protected groups dominate the program's management, a new group must have the support of the existing protected groups to receive funding. Such nonfeminist groups as Kids First! and REAL Women have been markedly unsuccessful in getting Court Challenges Program funding. Indeed, Monahan and Finkelstein (1993) suggest that the credibility and recognition the program confers on interest groups is as important to them as the program's funding.

In the future, the program might become an instrument for the existing protected groups to use in fending off new claims to section 15 status.

## GENERALIZABILITY

The Charter of Rights has not been around long enough to permit a full test of the Schelling Curve of Equality Rights Status. If the curve also applies to other status-seeking situations, such as human rights policies, then the history of Canada's human rights codes can be used to test it instead. Provincial and federal legislatures have used human rights codes to confer legislative status on certain groups in much the same way that the courts have used section 15 to confer constitutional status. The family of groups that receives protection under these human rights codes has expanded monotonically since Ontario established Canada's first human rights commission in 1962. Human rights codes in Canada now protect against discrimination on more than thirty different grounds (Knopff 1989, 36). Since there is a good collection of secondary sources on human rights legislation in Ontario (Howe 1991; Keene 1992; Knopff 1989; Sohn 1975), a loose test of the curve against Ontario's human rights legislation is in order.

The Schelling Curve of Equality Rights Status provides five general hypotheses about the competition for status:

1. The first time a given form of status is granted, several groups or individuals will share it.

A v-group must be established for a given form of status to be viable. As a result, when a new form of status is created, several members will share it.

2. Once a form of status is established, many other groups or individuals will try to get it.

After the v-group is established, a given form of status is valuable and therefore an attractive asset for other potential members of the v-group. Potential members will try to gain the status.

3. At some point, the number of new demands for the status will drop off.

As more groups or individuals gain a certain form of status, the value of gaining it begins to drop. After this point although non-status groups still have an incentive to seek status, some may find it more advantageous to invest their resources in other arenas.

4. Eventually, v-group members will actively oppose the attempts of new candidates to gain the status.

As the value of each member's share of a certain form of status drops, but before the net benefit of seeking that status disappears altogether, the members may begin to oppose the extension of status to new, potential members. In other words, they may act to protect the value of their status.

5. As the $v_2$-point is reached, members of the v-group may seek new, higher forms of status in order to trump new v-group members.

If it is possible for some members of the v-group to create a new and more elite form of status, they may do so instead of trying to deny new, potential members admission into the original v-group.

The Ontario Legislature has enacted a series of statutes prohibiting various forms of discrimination since World War II. For two decades before 1962, several pieces of legislation prohibited discrimination on certain grounds (ethnicity, religion, etc.) and in certain domains (notably private employment and accommodation).[17] In 1962 these statutes were consolidated into a single Ontario Human Rights Code and an Ontario Human Rights Commission was created to investigate complaints of discrimination. Where necessary, the Commission provides informal conciliation services or prosecutes cases before quasi-judicial boards of inquiry.

Several new groups have gained protected status under the Code since 1962. Two theories have been proposed to account for this growth, both predicting that the family of protected groups will expand forever. Flanagan (1985) suggests a bureaucratic politics theory. Following the theory that bureaucrats seek to extend their empires (Niskanen 1971), Flanagan notes that once human rights commissions are established with permanent staffs, the staffs stand to gain directly from the expansion of the number of grounds of prohibited discrimination. After all, every new ground provides more potential complaints for the staff to investigate. If the human rights bureaucrat's self-interest in enlarging his or her empire knows no bounds, then the expansion of human rights codes appears to be unbounded as well. Flanagan implies that the bureaucratic "manufacture of minorities" will continue ad infinitum. While interest group lobbying of government officials has some influence in the process of expanding human rights codes, the expansion is usually due to the "spontaneous recommendations of the commissions" themselves (Flanagan 1985, 120). Interest group activity may simply reinforce changes that would have happened anyway. The only brake on the expansion of human rights codes is its acceptability to the broader public opinion in Flanagan's account (121).

Yet, it is difficult to imagine governments giving scarce space on their legislative agendas to amending human rights codes if there is no interest group pressure for them. If commission staffs cannot gain interest group support to expand human rights guarantees, would human rights codes continue to expand? While bureaucratic self-interest plausibly explains much of the growth in human rights legislation, surely commission staffs must be careful to gain the support of a relevant interest group before pressing their expansionist agendas on political leaders. In turn, interest groups must see human rights code status as valuable before they sign up. So, where the self-interest of human rights bureaucrats begins to outstrip the self-interest of interest groups, the dynamics governing status seeking will define the limits of human rights legislation.

In a case study of Ontario, Howe (1991) sets out a second theory that is "complementary" (785) to Flanagan's. In his account, human rights legislation expands under pressure from Canada's reform liberal public philosophy and its implementation is subsequently slowed by the country's conservative liberal ethic. Awareness of the discrepancy between Canada's general liberal public philosophy and the practical reality of discrimination as a "contradiction of Canadian liberal values" inspires the pressures for expanding human rights codes. Now, Howe does not specify a precise mechanism that converts awareness into legislative outputs. Presumably interest group leaders publicize the value-practice discrepancy, and as awareness grows political entrepreneurs use the opportunity to gain popularity by expanding or strengthening the human rights codes. As long as there is a discrepancy between the public's commitment to equality and the reality of discrimination, and as long as someone continues to point it out, Howe's theory also predicts a continued expansion of human rights legislation.

If political pressure from a potentially protected group is necessary before legislators will expand the grounds of prohibited discrimination in human rights codes, then both Flanagan and Howe are incorrect to assume that the growth of such human rights codes will continue unbounded. In fact, in the future, the status of being protected in human rights codes may be so widely spread that currently protected groups will actively oppose the bids of other groups to have protection extended to them. This second v-point has not yet been reached in most Canadian jurisdictions, since gay and lesbian groups continue to seek the addition of sexual orientation to human rights codes, to build on their victories in several Canadian jurisdictions. Applying the Schelling Curve of Section 15 status to human rights codes shows that the pressure for expanding human rights codes should be self-limiting.

The scope of the Ontario Human Rights Code has expanded along four axes since its adoption in 1962. This complication produces a problem of control that prevents a rigorous test of the model. First, as already noted, the number of grounds of discrimination prohibited in the Code has expanded. Whereas the 1962 Code prohibited discrimination on the basis of ethnicity and religion, the current Code covers almost a dozen grounds of discrimination. Secondly, more organizations have been made subject to the Code. At first it applied only to large, private-sector firms, but it now applies to smaller businesses and the public sector as well. Thirdly, the definition of discrimination itself has expanded. In 1962 the Code only prohibited direct and intentional discrimination. Today it also outlaws systemic or indirect discrimination.[18] Finally, the powers of the commission and of boards of inquiry have expanded. The Schelling Curve model set out in Figure 4.5 isolates the first type of expansion, in the number of grounds of discrimination prohibited, from the other types of expansion in the Code. The other expansions of the Code have opened new ways to exploit protected status, and this increases $V_i$, the value of being included in the Code. The five hypotheses listed above should, however, apply to status-seeking politics over human rights legislation, with the proviso that 3 and 4 may be mitigated by expansions in the coverage of human rights legislation that increase $V_i$.

The history of Ontario's human rights legislation substantially confirms four of the five hypotheses. As outlined above, less-ambitious statutes preceded the Ontario Human Rights Code. Howe attributes this earlier legislation to the coalition-building activities of a small group of human rights activists, who created "coalitions of labour, minority, civil liberties and religious organizations . . . to gain specific laws . . . " (1991, 791). When the Ontario Human Rights Code was passed in 1962, it prohibited discrimination in a number of areas on the basis of race, creed, color, nationality, ancestry, or place of origin. The first Code, then, seems to have granted protected status to at least the minimum number of groups required to form a v-group, as predicted by hypothesis 1. This aspect of the Code's history bolsters the idea that status can be spread too narrowly to be viable.

Howe himself notes that "[no] sooner had the *Code* gone into effect than a reform movement arose for its expansion" (1991, 793). While there was pressure to expand the powers of the Commission and Boards of Inquiry, pressure also arose to add new grounds of discrimination. In 1972, the Code grew to prohibit discrimination on the basis of sex and marital status. New grounds of discrimination were also added in 1981, when as a result of a 1976 comprehensive review of Ontario's human rights legislation the Code was extensively revised. The Human Rights Commission and Boards of Inquiry were provided with new powers. The revision also added citizenship, age, family status, handicaps (both physical and mental), the receipt of public assistance, and record of offenses to the prohibited grounds of discrimination.[19] Finally, sexual orientation and pregnancy were added as prohibited grounds of discrimination in 1986.[20] Thus, once the Code came into existence, regular pressure seems to have arisen for adding new grounds of prohibited discrimination. This confirms the prediction of hypothesis 2.

The lengthy process of revising the Code begun in 1976 could explain the lull in expansion between 1972 and 1981. On the other hand, it could be that after the addition of sex and marital status in 1972 the family of groups given protected status by the Code was approaching the $v_2$-point. Other groups may only have found it in their interests to seek protected status again when the powers of the commission and of the boards of inquiry were expanded. In any case, since 1982 only two new grounds of discrimination have been added to the Code and none have been added since 1986.[21] Pressure for new grounds of discrimination has abated and it seems that the $v_2$ point has been reached, as predicted by $H_3$.

One of the model's predictions was not borne out. Protected groups did not actively oppose the extension of protected status to new groups in 1972, 1981 and 1986. Members of the v-group did not oppose the dilution of their status. On the other hand, protected groups did find higher forms of status to seek from Ontario legislators as hypothesis 5 predicts. Women's groups achieved a form of "trumping status" when Ontario adopted the Pay Equity Act.[22] This wide-ranging new type of human rights legislation regulated compensation in the public and private sectors in order to achieve equal pay for work of comparable value. Until the 1995 provincial election, Ontario was also implementing a comprehensive program of affirmative action for the public and private sectors aimed at increasing the representation of women, racial minorities, aboriginals (Indian, Inuit and Métis), and people with disabilities in the Ontario workforce. The groups targeted under the Ontario's affirmative action policies had achieved a higher form of human rights status. Where it is possible to create higher forms of status, it might be a convenient outlet for groups that would otherwise oppose expansions in the number of groups protected in a human rights code.

The history of the Ontario Human Rights Code generally conforms to the expectations generated by the Schelling Curve model in Figure 4.5. Since it is impossible to isolate the growth in the family of protected groups from the effects of other changes in the Code, it is impossible to make a more rigorous quantitative analysis.

## CONCLUSION

The Supreme Court has turned the Charter's equality rights section into a vehicle of status politics, a way to mete out different levels of status to different groups. By turning section 15 into a provision about hierarchy rather than equality, the Court put itself in the position of having to determine which groups deserve special status and which do not. The Court must favor some groups over others. And how has the Supreme Court decided to hand out this special status? By reading section 15 through the lens of the political disadvantage theory. It has decided to pick groups it thinks are historically disadvantaged in Canada and give them special protection in constitutional law.

What benefits flow from section 15 status? Consider the *Weatherall* case about the differential treatment of men and women serving sentences in federal prisons. There might be good policy reasons to treat men and women differently in prison. Cross-sex searches might be harder on women than men. But in upholding the policy, the Supreme Court's reasoning started at a different point. Under section 15 as the Supreme Court has interpreted it, men are not a disadvantaged group. Therefore, it is extremely difficult for a man to succeed in a claim of discrimination under section 15. Moreover, since there are many more men than women serving time in federal penitentiaries, a policy against all cross-sex searches would create less demand for female guards. This would hurt women, and the Court has recognized women with the status of "disadvantaged group." So, in principle, women can more easily make claims of sex discrimination under section 15.

*Weatherall* is not the only case where the courts have meted out different status to different groups. In *Boland* (1993), the Tax Court of Canada upheld the constitutionality of tax laws that discriminate against families with one parent staying at home to care for their children. Canadian tax law provides a benefit to parents making payments for the care of their children, but only if the payments are made to child care providers outside the family. The benefit is not available to a parent that pays his or her spouse to remain at home to care for his or her children. The court applied the Supreme Court's equality rights rules and found that "stay-at-home spouses" are not a "vulnerable group" in today's society. They have not been "subject historically to discrimination" and are not a "discrete and insular minority" (Boland 1993, 1560). Therefore, tax laws that extend benefits based on a spouse's work choices do not violate the Charter's equality rights guarantees.

The Supreme Court has put the country's courts on a dangerous path here. The Sopinka trilogy of intervention cases forced the Court to create a hierarchy by giving some groups preferential treatment when they apply for leave to intervene. Similarly, the Court's section 15 cases have forced it to create a hierarchy by giving some groups preferential treatment in equality rights cases. Constitutional status may be a long Canadian tradition. Catholic, Protestant, anglophone, and francophone minorities have enjoyed special constitutional rights since Confederation. But just as the Supreme Court has handed out special status to certain groups in court cases, so Canada's first ministers tried to hand out special status in the Meech Lake and Charlottetown Accords. The battles over relative group status in those proposed constitutional amendments played themselves out quickly, and showed how inherently conflictual and potentially damaging the politics of status seeking is, especially when it is played out in the high-stakes constitutional realm. *Weatherall* and *Boland* are just the beginning of the politics of status playing itself out in the courtroom.

# 5

## POLITICAL DISADVANTAGE
## AND STATE ACTION

Most scholars writing on interest group litigation assume that the groups involved in litigation emerge from the private sphere, or "society," to represent interests in opposition, or at least in tension, to the state. This view matches a wider perspective that judicial review, especially in the civil liberties field, is essentially a battle between state and social actors. Both these ideas underlie the political disadvantage theory of interest group litigation and the concept of the disadvantaged group. In the past thirty years, political scientists have qualified if not abandoned the society-centered and pluralist assumptions that underlie these traditional views of judicial review and interest group litigation. Neo-institutionalism has drawn attention to the state's role in shaping society, and therefore its political environment. Other work on interest groups has questioned the assumption that groups emerge spontaneously from society to represent interests in society. These two strands of analysis converge to call into question the view of judicial review as a conflict between societal and state actors. If the state has encouraged the expansion of judicial review, then judicial review is not simply about adjudicating disputes between private interests and the state. If the state has encouraged the creation of

99

certain groups, and encouraged them to pursue their political objectives in the courts, then the view that interest group litigation is about societal interests emerging from society to challenge government action cannot be accurate. Moreover, the political disadvantage theory fails to capture the complexity of the situation.

This chapter begins to sketch the extent of government involvement in expanding interest group litigation and judicial review in Canada. The Canadian government has established many channels to encourage interest group litigation. A full discussion is impossible here. This chapter shows how the federal government has encouraged interest groups to litigate in the pursuit of their political objectives, through the Court Challenges Program. The CCP was created in the late 1970s as part of the federal campaign against the Parti Québécois' language legislation. In the mid-1980s, the Mulroney government made a bid for the support of socially progressive voters by extending the program into the equality rights field. As the program has matured, its interest group clients came to play a direct role in its management. The networks of interest groups that the CCP created were strong enough to undo the federal government's 1992 decision to cancel the program altogether, and have played a direct role in its management and funding decisions.

This article does not argue that the Court Challenges Program created interest group litigation in Canada. As noted in the Introduction, political and community interests have long used the courts to advance their aims. Even the new, systematic appellate interest group litigation this book has documented is not entirely the product of federal action. Nevertheless, both federal and provincial governments have supported this new type of litigation in Canada. The government involvement in encouraging this new type of litigation raises questions about the traditional view of judicial review and interest group litigation. This, in turn, raises questions about the concept of the disadvantaged group.

## THE TRADITIONAL VIEW OF JUDICIAL REVIEW AND INTEREST GROUP LITIGATION

Most of the literature on judicial review, especially on judicial review under the Charter of Rights, views the phenomenon in traditional terms: as a way to resolve disputes between governments and private actors. In the classical liberal view, judicial review protects private, individual rights against state action. A more collectivist view sees judicial review securing the rights of private actors to various kinds of state action. Both schools of thought assume that judicial review pits governments against private litigants. Retired Supreme Court judge Bertha Wilson endorsed such an analysis when she claimed that, under the Charter, "the courts have become mediators between the state and the individual" (Wilson 1986, 239). Under the Charter, she has written, the courts have been given "the task of developing some kind of balance between the fundamental rights of citizens . . . and the right and obligation of democratically elected governments to govern . . . " (Wilson 1988, 371).

It is but a short step from this view to the idea that interest group litigation pits private actors against the state. For example, in the mid-1980s Jillian Welch urged the Supreme Court to accept interest group interveners as regular participants in appeals. She based her argument on the assumption that these groups are private actors. "In the Charter era, judicial review no longer engages only the interests of two levels of government . . . but also the interests of a somewhat mysterious third entity, that of the 'individual'. . . . " Since Charter cases engage the interest of both individuals and governments, "representatives of both the 'individual writ large' and the government are required" (Welch 1985, 225). Interest groups, in Welch's view, represent the individual writ large. In constitutional litigation, "the role that can be played by an interest group is qualitatively the same as the role played by the attorney-general . . . " (226). Interest group litigation thus helps to achieve the Charter's promise of checking government action.

Two assumptions underpin this traditional view of interest group litigation and judicial review. First, if judicial review and interest group litigation are essentially battles between private actors and the state, there must be a sharp distinction between state and society. Secondly, if interest groups simply represent their members, they must emerge naturally from society to represent political interests. These assumptions also underpin the political disadvantage theory and the concept of the disadvantaged group. What is a disadvantaged group but a vehicle for private citizens who are in conflict with the government and who cannot use normal political avenues to influence the government to band together and battle the government in court?

If the society-centered and pluralist assumptions underlying these views of interest group litigation are correct, then interest group litigation indeed serves the traditional view of judicial review by being a check on the state. The political disadvantage theory is not challenged. However, what if government itself plays an important role in forming and maintaining many of the groups involved in litigation? Is such interest group litigation a purely "grassroots" or "bottom-up" phenomenon? If Canadian interest group litigation has been in part state sponsored, can the traditional view of judicial review and interest group litigation still hold?

## CHALLENGES TO THE TRADITIONAL VIEW

In the past two decades, political scientists have focused new attention on the state's role in politics. This institutionalist literature shows how the state can act as an independent actor. It can pursue policies that diverge from the preferences of society and social groups. The salient points can be gleaned in the writings of Theda Skocpol. Fifteen years ago, she wrote of "macroscopic" analysis of politics that emphasizes "the ways in which the structure and activities of states unintentionally influence the formation of groups and the political capacities, ideas and demands of various sectors of society" (Skocpol 1985, 21). The state is not simply "an actor whose independent efforts may need to be taken more seriously than heretofore in accounting for policy making and social change" (21). Instead, the state's "organizational configurations" and "overall patterns of activity" allow certain political issues to emerge and not others. More recently, she has developed a "polity-centred approach" to highlight the impact that state and party organizations can have on the identities and goals of the social groups involved in policy making (Skocpol 1992). The state shapes its own political environment. Any particular set of political demands may be the product of earlier state action rather than a reflection of a preexisting preference of societal actors.

In Canada, Alan Cairns is most notably associated with this line of thought. His thinking about the state has shifted in important

ways over the past twenty years.[1] His early work on the state looked
at Canadian society and its relations with eleven competing, coher-
ent, federal and provincial Leviathans (Cairns 1977). Increased competition between these eleven governments was fragmenting society,
he argued. When Cairns shifted his attention to the impact of the
1982 constitutional reform, he refined his earlier ideas about the
state. He now sees a more blurred picture of state-society relations.
The state is fragmented, and "embedded" in an equally fragmented
society (Cairns 1985). It has many nodes, each closely connected to
an interested public. These nodes shape their fragments of society
and are in turn shaped by them. Fragments of the state enlist fragments of society in battles against other state fragments. Political
scientists, he concludes, "must learn to think in terms of politicized
societies caught in webs of interdependence with the state, and we
must think of the latter as an embedded state tied down by its
multiple linkages with society..." (Cairns 1985, 55).

At the macro level, institutionalist work such as Skocpol's and
Cairns's blurs the distinction between state and society. Political
demands often reflect state action. In the past three decades, complementary midrange research has undermined pluralist theories of
interest group activities. Whereas pluralists once assumed that interest groups formed to represent all interests in society (Bentley 1967
[1908]; Truman 1951), recent work demonstrates how difficult it
is for interest groups to form at all. They face serious hurdles to
mobilizing collective action (Olson 1971 [1965])". Group leaders
must design ways to overcome these hurdles (Salisbury 1969). In
many instances, leaders create public interest groups, or "citizen"
groups, by locating wealthy patrons to fund their startup costs and
then finding members to join the groups (Walker 1983). Not all
interests form groups, and group members do not automatically
control the groups that do form. The interests of group leaders may
not be identical with those of members. In Canada, governments
actively sponsor a variety of interest groups (McCartney 1990).

LEAF's history, for example, demonstrates this postpluralist
work on interest groups. As outlined in chapter 2, LEAF emerged
from a loose coalition of activists in groups such as the Ad Hoc
Committee of Women on the Constitution, the Charter of Rights
Committee, and the Charter of Rights Education Foundation. A
small group of experienced feminist activists (Mary Eberts, Beth

Atcheson, Beth Symes, Marilou McPhedran, Nancy Jackman, and Kathleen O'Neil) met in August 1984, to put together a feminist litigation fund for Canada. The group was "well-versed in the arts of grant applications" (Razack 1991, 43). In October, the month that the CACSW report *Women and Legal Action* was released, the group received a $100,000 grant from Nancy Jackman's family foundation to get started. O'Neil soon had a $117,000 grant from her organization, the Federation of Women's Teachers' Associations of Ontario (Razack 1991, 47). By November, the core of LEAF activists had raised an additional $50,000 from the Jackman Foundation, and $700 in other donations. According to Razack, "every conceivable network was activated in the interests of finding the financial support for LEAF" (46). The rest of 1984 was occupied with "grant applications" and appeals to "wealthy women" (47). The organization came together in early 1985 and soon received a $1 million endowment from the Ontario government. Government funding has accounted for about half of LEAF's budget since then (Razack 1991, 54, fn. 7). Patron funding has always been critical to LEAF's work.

These twin ideas—the institutionalist observation that political demands result from prior state action, and the postpluralist one that interest groups form in complex ways—challenge the underpinnings of the traditional views of judicial review and interest group litigation. They raise doubts about whether interest group litigation is a battle between societal interests facing an oppressive or hostile government. They suggest that the traditional view of judicial review may be too simplistic. These twin ideas are of particular interest in Canada, where the federal citizenship programs have been deeply involved in creating networks of interest groups and keeping them operating.

## THE SECRETARY OF STATE AND INTEREST GROUPS

Leslie Pal weaves together these twin ideas in his comprehensive analysis of the Canadian government's "citizenship programs" (1993). The federal government first established citizenship programs in the postwar years to make Canadians aware of the benefits and responsibilities of citizenship. It did this by supporting community groups with small project grants and maintaining links to Canada's voluntary sector (Pal 1993, 150). This effort carried a low profile for two decades following the war, but it was "a ripe candidate for enhancement when politicians began to cast about for a larger cultural and community role for the federal state" a few years later (Pal 1993, 97).

After the 1968 federal election, the Trudeau government's "Just Society" agenda gave the citizenship programs a new strategic importance. Trudeau's desire to promote "citizen participation" and his plans to combat Quebec nationalism led the federal government to shape Canada's interest group networks more directly. The Just Society pushed the Secretary of State beyond its passive support for community projects. To demonstrate that French-speaking communities outside Quebec could survive and thrive, Ottawa established a policy toward "official language minority groups" (OLMGs). Cabinet authorized a new Social Action Program in the Secretary of State's Department to "animate" French-Canadian minorities, deliberately mobilizing "social sentiments" in "desired directions" (Pal 1993, 103). The Branch began to provide funding and professional organizers to mobilize French Canadian minority associations. After the 1971 report of the Royal Commission on the Status of Women, similar support flowed to women's groups. Trudeau's 1971 policy statement on multiculturalism gave the department the task of supporting ethnic groups as well. By 1972, the Secretary of State had a broad mandate to mobilize Canadian society by funding OLMGs, multicultural groups, feminist groups, immigrants, Natives, and youth.

The federal government's enthusiasm for these citizenship programs lagged after the 1972 federal election. The multiculturalism program was redirected to secure the Liberal Party's electoral fortunes. Other Just Society groups turned out to be as often the adversaries as the allies of the federal government. The 1970 Quebec election of Robert Bourassa's federalist government in Quebec seemed to end Canada's regime crisis (Pal 1993, 118–121). These programs carried on through inertia and the support they received from their new constituents. Their fate was buffeted by the government's external political environment, with their importance rising and falling with the broader challenges to the government. When a separatist government took office in Quebec in 1976 and plunged the country into a new regime crisis, the federal government responded by reinvigorating its support for linguistic minorities. Pal notes that the Women's Program took on more importance with the UN's International Women's Year in 1975, and during the constitutional patriation process in 1980 and 1981. Multiculturalism's electoral importance remained constant.

Pal concludes that in the end, the federal government could rarely use its citizenship programs in a deliberate effort to shape its political environment. Rather, the state "was at least as much a captive of these programs as were its purported clients" (Pal 1993, 150). The federal government did use its sponsorship of interest groups to enlist them in its short-term objectives. Yet, over the long term, the citizenship programs have shaped Canada's identity and rights politics in subtle ways. They have amplified the importance of identity politics and collective rights seeking in Canada's politics. They have augmented claims for substantive equality. Pal concludes that the Secretary of State has influenced the universe of Canadian interest groups in far-reaching ways.

## GOVERNMENT SUPPORT FOR INTEREST GROUP LITIGATION

The Secretary of State has also played a direct role in encouraging interest group litigation in Canada through the Court Challenges Program. The program originally was created as part of the Trudeau government's response to the Parti Québécois' agenda on language and sovereignty association.[2] It served the Liberal program on national unity and language rights by encouraging groups to enlist the courts in their battles against provincial language laws. In 1985, the Mulroney government wanted to appeal to socially progressive voters without creating expensive new entitlement programs. It therefore expanded the program to fund equality rights challenges to federal legislation and gave the CCP an autonomous organization. In the years that followed, the CCP's managers actively created networks of interest groups and encouraged new groups to pursue public interest litigation. Over time, these networks of groups became increasingly involved in running the program. In the 1992 federal budget, the program fell victim to the Mulroney government's renewed fiscal agenda and the growing concerns of social conservatives in his caucus about its funding decisions. The program's interest group supporters mobilized a vocal campaign to reestablish the CCP. After the 1993 election, the Liberal government re-created the Program and invited its main beneficiaries to assist their efforts.

*Phase I—The Origins of the Court Challenges Program*

When the Parti Québécois won the 1976 Quebec election on a promise to hold a referendum on sovereignty-association for Quebec, the country was plunged into a deep regime crisis. Moreover, the PQ then introduced language legislation, Bill 101, and challenged Trudeau's strategy of countering Quebec nationalism with national bilingualism. The federal Liberals responded to these developments by redoubling their support for bilingualism. Since bilingualism had proceeded as far as possible in the federal jurisdiction, attention turned to promoting bilingualism at the provincial level. In 1977, the government expanded its support for OLMGs and encouraged OLMGs to lobby the provinces for more bilingual programs (Brodie 1992, 134).

The federal government realized that few provinces would expand their bilingualism programs voluntarily. The PQ was committed to its language legislation and other provinces saw reason to expand their French language services. Trudeau had long realized that he would need to enlist the courts as allies to implement bilingualism at the provincial level. Before entering politics, he had written that it would not be "very realistic to rely upon goodwill or purely political action" to expand language services.[3] In October 1977, the federal cabinet met to discuss the PQ's language legislation. It considered challenging Bill 101 directly, either by disallowing it or by asking the Supreme Court to rule on the constitutionality of several provisions. Trudeau decided that a confrontation would help the PQ in its planned sovereignty-association referendum.[4] Instead, the federal government decided to wait for private citizens to challenge Bill 101 and then intervene to support their arguments. In the spring of 1978, when such private challenges were not forthcoming, Secretary of State John Roberts and Justice Minister Ron Basford established the Court Challenges Program to offer financial support to challenges of provincial language legislation in several provinces including Quebec (Canada 1989, 3). Creating interest group litigation against provincial laws avoided the potential pitfalls of a direct attack on Bill 101. Between 1978 and 1982, the new program funded six cases, three challenges to parts of Bill 101 and three cases in Manitoba and Saskatchewan. When Trudeau secured new language guarantees in the Charter of Rights, the CCP was expanded to follow suit (Canada 1989, 4). By 1984–1985, the program, which was still under the administration of the Secretary of State, had an annual budget of $200,000 (Canada 1985, 133).

Since OLMGs and the federal government agreed on what the CCP would try to achieve, there was no need for the program to be administered autonomously. It was integrated into the government's broader efforts to support groups lobbying for bilingualism in the provinces. Between 1978 and August 1985, five out of the twenty-two cases that had received or applied for funding had also had help from the Secretary of State's main fund for language groups, the Official Languages Community Program (Canada 1989, 5). These numbers may be small, but most cases were only in the early stages of development or litigation by 1985. Karwacki concludes that at this stage, "the executive created a legal funding branch that complemented and reinforced legislated bilingualism" (Karwacki 1994, 77). The Court Challenges Program had become the legal action branch of the federal government's attack on the PQ's program.

*Phase II—Program Expansion*

In 1985, the Charter's equality rights section was about to come into force. An array of interest groups who were already being funded by the Secretary of State were mobilizing to take advantage of it. Governments had given themselves three years to ensure their legislation complied with the equality rights, but few of these groups thought the statute audit process had been vigorous enough. They saw the federal government's remedial legislation as superficial and cosmetic, and were frustrated by Justice Minister

John Crosbie's unwillingness to take a "substantive" interpretation of the Charter's equality rights (Karwacki 1994, 49). Consequently, they began to mobilize for extensive public interest litigation. In early 1985, the House of Commons struck a Committee on Equality Rights to investigate the implications of section 15. The groups mobilizing for litigation feared that they would not have the financial resources to match other interests in court, so they used the Commons committee as a forum to demand government funding for their litigation.[5] In effect, they wanted an equality rights counterpart to the OLMG-oriented Court Challenges Program. Since these groups suspected the government did not share their view of how equality rights should shape federal policies, they wanted this funding to flow through an independent organization.

At the same time, the new Mulroney government was looking for a way to promote a progressive agenda on social issues without creating new entitlement programs.[6] An expanded Court Challenges Program fit this need. On September 25, 1985, before the Committee on Equality Rights had an opportunity to recommend federal government funding for equality rights litigation, Crosbie and Secretary of State Benoit Bouchard announced the expansion of the Court Challenges Program into the area of equality rights. The new CCP would be allowed to fund equality rights challenges to federal policies and legislation. The ministers also granted the program some independence by hiring the Canadian Council on Social Development (CCSD) to administer it.[7] The program's budget was set at $9 million over five years.

The response from interest group leaders was lukewarm. While they were happy to have additional government funding for their litigation, they had two concerns about the new CCP (Karwacki 1994, 55–56). First, they wanted more say over the program's funding decisions. The federal government planned to retain a veto over the composition of the program's governing council. It looked as though the CCP would therefore be subject to the government's control. Secondly, the program had no budget for community outreach. These groups wanted the program to help mobilize their own supporters and draw allied organizations into Charter litigation. As chapter 4 suggests, they likely also wanted to limit the number of new groups drawn into Charter litigation.

As it turned out, the concerns were misplaced. The federal government did not try to control the CCP's work. CCSD brought in activists from the equality-seeking groups and the OLMGs to sit on advisory councils and to determine which cases would be funded. Since the government did not explicitly define the program's objectives, its management actively shaped its own clientele (Bureau of Management Consulting 1989, 35). The CCP's granting decisions therefore reflected the views of the equality-seeking groups and the OLMGs. For example, the CCP funded many cases by the Women's Legal Education and Action Fund (LEAF), including its pro-choice intervention in the *Borowski* abortion case. Yet, it refused to fund REAL Women's pro-life intervention in the same case, claiming that REAL Women's position in the case would not advance the cause of substantive equality for women.

Moreover, the CCP pursued an extensive program of community outreach. It actively encouraged new groups to pursue equality and language litigation. It held meetings to create networks of equality-seeking groups and OLMGs, and in some cases to create new groups. In 1989/1990, spending on community outreach took up 15 percent of the program's overall budget (Bureau of Management Consulting 1989, 9). Spending on mobilization grew sharply after 1987/1988, when the program decided to begin to seek out cases actively (Bureau of Management Consulting 1989, 25). It began sponsoring workshops and meetings that created new equality rights groups and, in turn, generated new cases. In 1988/1989, the program spent $1,421 on "Public Information" for each application that it received, more than ten times what it spent deciding which applications to fund.[8] Once it received an application, the program created support networks of people involved in similar cases. The program managers mobilized and consolidated networks of the groups involved in language and equality rights litigation.

When the CCP was set to expire at the end of March 1990, the groups that had originally sought equality rights funding lobbied hard for its renewal. This is not surprising. The CCP had begun to campaign for its renewal long before it set to expire. When it organized the First National Meeting of Equality-Seeking Groups in January 1989, the groups in attendance struck a com-

mittee to communicate their "unanimous support" for the program to the federal government. They expressed their "keen interest in ensuring that the program's mandate be renewed" (Court
Challenges Program 1989–1990, 12). The House of Commons
Standing Committee on Human Rights and the Status of Disabled
Persons was mandated to review the program in the second half
of 1989. It heard from twenty-four delegations—three composed
of officials from the CCP, members of its Community Advisory
panel, and staff of the CCSD, and twelve from groups that had
received program funding.[9] The "virtually unanimous" message
from the witnesses was "that the reasons for continuation are not
merely sufficient, but compelling" (Canada 1989, 23). In the end,
the committee recommended renewing and expanding the program. Moreover, it recommended broadening the CCP to fund
more kinds of cases and to include explicit funding for community
mobilization. Although the government rejected most of the
committee's recommendations, it did renew the program and gave
it a five-year budget of $12 million. The government also en-
trusted the program's administration to the Human Rights Centre
at the University of Ottawa.[10]

### Phase III—Cancellation and Renewal

When the Mulroney government cancelled the Court Challenges
Program in its 1992 budget, the strength of the networks the
CCP had developed became clear. The 1992 budget saw the re-
invigoration of the government's fiscal restraint agenda. The
program's cancellation was part of a broader cost-cutting effort
that saw several other programs wound up (Brodie 1992, 225). At
the same time, social conservatives on the government backbenches
had become concerned with the social reform agenda the program
supported. Multiculturalism and Citizenship Minister Gerry Weiner
said that while the program had been effective, it had established
"a solid base of jurisprudence for future years," and that the issues
could be left in the hands of the provinces. Justice Minister Kim
Campbell said the government would continue to support Charter
challenges, but would do so in more cost-effective ways. The
cancellation outraged groups that had received funding from the
program. "We offended the powerful groups," said Kathleen Ruff,

a CCP official. "It is a terrible loss for our communities," according to Raymond Bisson, president of the Federation of Francophones Outside Quebec.[11] Bertha Wilson joined the campaign by sending an open letter to Justice Minister Kim Campbell calling the program "imaginative and worthwhile" (Canada 1992, 47–48). The chief commissioner of the Canadian Human Rights Commission cited the cancellation of the program as evidence that the government acted as if human rights were expendable.[12] Since the courts are so involved in human rights issues, "we should at least make adequate provision for their use," he wrote. "In this light, the decision to cut the Court Challenges Program could only be perceived by equality-seeking groups as adding insult to injury. . . . For many individuals and groups [it was] the only way to have the public authorities acknowledge the substance of their rights" (Canadian Human Rights Commission 1993, 16). The Commissioner of Official Languages was "surprised and disturbed" by the cancellation. The program has been "essential to the clarification and development of constitutional language rights in Canada" (Commissioner of Official Languages 1993, 24). The Commissioner also commissioned a report to document how many areas of language rights in Canada still awaited judicial clarification (Goreham 1992).

There was a strong outcry against the government's decision, and the networks the program had built were able to take advantage of that to reverse the government's decision. Within two weeks of the budget, the House of Commons Standing Committee on Human Rights and the Status of Disabled Persons began hearings into the cancellation. The committee heard from eight delegations: two from program officials, two from its interest group beneficiaries, two from the federal government, the Canadian Human Rights Commission and the Canadian Bar Association (CBA). All but the federal delegations supported renewing the program. The committee's report urged the government to reconstitute the program as an independent foundation. "Without a program such as Court Challenges, access to the remedies available under the Charter will probably only be assured to groups and individuals in Canadian society that already have financial and political advantages" (Canada 1992, 5). Furthermore, cancelling the program hurt the cases that were already under way. Many were only at the trial level and would be subject to an appeal. "The private litigant, already functioning from a position of disadvantage, will be left with attempting to raise funds to defend the appeal" (Canada 1992, 7). The committee's members concluded: "We cannot over-emphasize the value of collaboration and cooperation, particularly in the fundamental task of assisting all Canadians to gain access to *their* Constitution and to *their* Charter" (12). They urged the government to endow an independent Court Challenges Foundation with $10 million.

The program's supporters continued their campaign and turned the CCP's cancellation into an election issue (Karwacki 1994, 71–72). They convinced both the Liberal and PC parties to include promises to reinstate the program in their election platforms. Jean Chretien promised to reestablish the Court Challenges Program on June 8, 1993, and then appeared before the program's Equality Rights Advisory Committee in the fall to reiterate the promise. The promise appeared in the Liberal's Red Book of election commitments. Again, the promise was a low-cost way to appeal to socially progressive voters, and in keeping with the party's traditional support for Charter rights discourse. Kim Campbell reversed her own position on the program in August 1993. As a government minister, she supported the decision to cut the CCP. As prime minister, she promised to create a new Charter Law Development Fund after the election. Karwacki lists three possible explanations for Campbell's about-face (Karwacki 1994, 72). One possibility is that Campbell may have needed an election plank to make her more palatable to the activist population in her Vancouver riding. A second explanation is the vigorous lobbying campaign launched by the program's beneficiaries. Finally, the support of state actors such as the standing committee and the Commissioners of Official Languages and Human Rights also embarrassed the government. In any case, after the election Allan Rock, the new Liberal minister of justice used his first public speech in office to promise the reestablishment of the program,[13] and the promise was repeated in the government's first Throne Speech.

Following the election, Heritage Minister Michel Dupuy told the program's supporters that they would decide how to structure and administer the renewed program. The government hired a private consulting firm to consult the program's intended interest group beneficiaries, legal academics, and the CBA on the renewal of the CCP (Price Waterhouse 1994). Nineteen representatives attended a consultative meeting organized by the consultants—five from official language groups the program had funded, including François Boileau of the Fédération des communautés francophones et acadiens (FCFA), nine from equality-seeking and other groups the Program had funded, including Shelagh Day of LEAF, one from the CBA, and four academics, including Lynn Smith from the University of British Columbia Law School and Fernand Landry of the Université de Moncton. These representatives immediately used the consultation to claim an ongoing role in running the renewed program. They started by rejecting the set of objectives that the government had set for the new CCP, and drafted a set of objectives that recognized the historical inequality of disadvantaged groups and official language minorities. Then, they set down the parameters for the new program's budget, administration, and structure. Finally, they ensured they would have a role in running the corporation that would administer the new program. OLMGs, equality rights groups, and the CBA would appoint the first board of directors. Panels composed of OLMG activists, equality rights activists, and legal academics would make all funding decisions.

The new Court Challenges Program was incorporated in October 1994, and immediately signed a three-year funding agreement with the federal government guaranteeing the new program $2.75 million annually. The new program's board of directors was chaired by Fernand Landry and included two long-time language rights activists and two experienced equality rights activists. The board in turn recruited Boileau to be the executive director of the new organization, and named two decision-making panels filled with language rights and equality rights activists. The language rights panel's first chair was Marc Godbout, a former FCFA executive director. The first co-chairs of the equality rights panel were Shelagh Day and Ken Norman, a member of the equality rights panel from the former program.

This history of the program leads to four salient points. First, starting in 1985, the Court Challenges Program reached out to mobilize groups around legal action. It formed and shaped net-

**Table 5.1** CCP Interventions in the Supreme Court, 1984–1993

| Intervener | Cases Funded by C.C.P. | Funding |
|---|---|---|
| *Women's Legal Education and Action Fund** | *Law Society of B.C. v Andrews* (1989)** | $15,350 |
| | | 34,000 |
| | *Borowski* (1981) | unknown |
| | *Taylor* (1990) | unknown |
| | *Andrews* (1990) | unknown |
| | *Keegstra* (1990) | 35,000 |
| | *Seaboyer* (1991) | unknown |
| | *Schacter* (1992) | |
| *Women's League Education and Action Fund** with: Barbara Schlifer Commemorative Clinic, Broadside Communications, Metro Action Committee on Public Violence Against Women, Metro Toronto Special Committee on Child Abuse, Ontario Coalition of Rape Crisis Centres, Women's College Hospital Sexual Assault Care Team, Women HealthSharing* | *Canadian Newspapers* (1988) | 35,000 |
| *L'Association francaise des conseils scolaires de l'Ontario* | *Ref re: Bill 30 (Ont. Separate School Funding* (1987) | unknown |
| *L'Association francaise des conseils scolaires de l'Ontario with:* L'Association des Enseignant(e)s francophone de l'Ontario and L'Association Canadienne-francaise de l'Ontario* | *Mahé* (1990) | unknown |
| *L'Association culturelle francaise-canadienne de Saskatchewan* | *Mercure* (1988) | 51,500 |
| *Coalition of Provincial Organizations of the Handicapped** | *Law Society of B. C. v Andrews* (1989)** | 35,000 |
| *Quebec Association of Protestant School Boards* | *Mahé* (1990) | unknown |

*(continued)*

**Table 5.1** CCP Interventions in the Supreme Court,
1984–1883 *(continued)*

| Intervener | Cases Funded by C.C.P. | Funding |
|---|---|---|
| *Canadian Disability Rights Council\* with:* Cdn Association for Community Living\*, Cdn Mental Health Association\* | *Swain* (1991) | 35,000 |
| *EGALE with:* Canadian Rights and Liberties Federation\*, National Action Committee on the Status of Women\*, National Association of Women and the Law\* | *Mossop* (1993) | unknown |
| *Canadian Council for Refugees* | *Ward* (1992) | unknown |
| *Alliance Quebec\** | *Reference re: Man Language Rights* (1992) | unknown |
| | *Sinclair* (1992) | unknown |
| *Fédération des francophones hors Québec/Fédération des communautés et acadiennes\** | *Reference re: Man Lang. Rights* (1992) | unknown |
| Total Interventions | | 35 |
| Confirmed Funding | | $265,850 |
| Estimated Total Funding | | $650,850 |

*Notes:*
  \* indicates a recipient of Secretary of State funding at least one year
    between 1982/1983 and 1992/1993.
  \*\* LEAF and COPOH received CCP funds to research equality rights issues
    in preparation for the *Andrews* case.

*Source:* C.C.P. files released under the *Access to Information Act* and *Public Accounts of Canada,* 1982/1983 to 1992/1993.

works of these groups. Secondly, several of the groups involved in the CCP also benefited from the Secretary of State's citizenship programs. They already had a base of government funds and support. Thirdly, the networks the CCP formed campaigned successfully to undo the 1992 decision to cancel the program. Finally, after 1985, the program gradually became more autonomous from the government. After 1997, its beneficiaries have controlled the program.

## The Court Challenges Program's Impact

The federal government intended to encourage interest group litigation through the CCP. Was the program decisive in allowing interest groups to litigate in Canada? Definitive proof is impossible. However, the program did provide important support to cases that might not otherwise have gone ahead. First, the CCP spent time and money on outreach programs. It formed and shaped networks of groups. It either helped convince some groups of the benefits of going to court or it aided their litigation. Secondly, the CCP has supported many litigation efforts. For example, the program has funded a significant number of interventions before the Supreme Court of Canada, especially interventions by public interest groups. Table 5.1 shows the Supreme Court interventions funded by the Court Challenges Program between 1984 and 1993. Table 5.2 shows the number of nongovernment interventions in

**Table 5.2** Nongovernment Interventions
and CCP Funding, 1984–1993

| Type of Intervener | Interventions | |
|---|---|---|
| | Interventions | # Funded |
| *Economic Interests:* | 64 | 2 |
| *Public Interests:* | 128 | 28 |
| Rights Organizations | 47 | 13 |
| Language Groups | 30 | 9 |
| Other Public Interest Groups | 24 | 6 |
| Religious Groups | 11 | 0 |
| Abortion Groups | 6 | 0 |
| Ethnic Groups | 7 | 0 |
| Environmental Groups | 2 | 0 |
| Native Groups | 1 | 0 |
| *Individuals:* | 36 | 0 |
| *Other Groups:* | 2 | 0 |
| Total | 230 | 30 |

*Source:* Supreme Court Reports, 1984–1993 and C.C.P. files released under the *Access to Information Act.*

the Supreme Court between 1984 and 1993, the first ten years of the Court's Charter cases. Fifteen percent of these interventions received funding from the CCP.[14] Few economic interests received CCP funding, and individuals have received none, but 22 percent of public interest interveners had Court Challenges program funding. The program backed almost one-third of interventions by

**Table 5.3** Court Challenges Program Cases
in the Supreme Court, 1984–1993

| Case | Parties with CCP Funding |
| --- | --- |
| *Bilodeau* (1986) | Bilodeau |
| *MacDonald* (1986) | MacDonald |
| *Societés des Acadiens* (1986) | Société des Acadiens |
| *Mercure* (1988) | Mercure |
| *Ford* (1988) | Ford et al., funded through Alliance Quebec |
| *Mahé* (1990) | Assn de l'ecole Georges et Julia Bugnet |
| *Sheldon S.* (1990) | Sheldon S. funded through Canadian Foundation for Children and the Law |
| *Tétrault-Gadoury* (1991) | Tétrault-Gadoury |
| *Canadian Council of Churches* (1992) | Canadian Council of Churches |
| *Reference re: Manitoba Language Rights* (1985) | cases giving rise to the reference funded at lower courts |
| *Mossop* (1993) | Mossop funded at lower courts |
| *Schacter* (1992) | Schacter |
| *Reference re: Public Schools Act (Manitoba)* (1993) | cases giving rise to the reference funded at lower courts |
| *Sauvé v. Queen* | both appellants funded at lower courts |
| *Symes* (1993) | Symes funded at lower courts |
| Total cases | 15 |

*Source:* C.C.P. files released under the *Access to Information Act*.

language groups, as well as about one-quarter of those by rights groups and other public interest groups.

Interventions represent only part of the interest group activity at the Supreme Court. Interest groups can also launch cases themselves, or sponsor "test cases" by individuals. To get a fuller picture of the CCP's role in funding interest group litigation before the Supreme Court, Table 5.3 lists the fifteen Charter cases before the Supreme Court between 1984 and 1993 that were launched with CCP funding. The program backed almost every language rights case the Court heard during this time. It also funded several of the Court's equality rights cases. Although the program could not fund interventions in the Supreme Court's leading equality rights case, *Law Society of BC v Andrews*, because the case concerned a provincial and not a federal law, it did fund the legal research that both LEAF and COPOH used in the case.[15]

What policy impact have the CCP's cases had? Again, looking only at cases that reached the Supreme Court, the program had an effect in both of its target areas of the law. On language rights, the program mobilized OLMGs to take legal action against the provinces and local authorities. The effect is clearest in Manitoba. The 1870 Manitoba Act provided good legal grounds for French Canadians to challenge the province's 1890 Official Languages Act as soon as the act was adopted. The Secretary of State's citizenship programs began supporting OLMGs such as the Société franco-manitobaine in the late 1960s. Yet, the challenges to Manitoba's language legislation never reached the Supreme Court until the CCP started to fund language cases.[16] In other language cases supported by the CCP, Canadian courts have steadily expanded entitlements to bilingual services and minority language education at the provincial and local levels. The leading language rights precedents have been mostly set in cases with CCP money.

The program's track record on equality rights cases is more mixed, but these cases have been more wide-ranging. The CCP's funding has promoted the substantive, rather that the formal, view of equality rights advanced by groups such as LEAF.[17] For example, when it became clear that the Supreme Court's decision in *Andrews v. Law Society of B.C.* would set the overall framework of precedent for the interpretation of equality rights in Canada, the CCP funded the legal research that LEAF and COPOH used in their interventions in the case. Their arguments for a substantive approach seem to have influenced the Supreme Court and helped to set the overall framework for equality rights jurisprudence since (Hausegger 2000). The program also funded the parties to the *Schacter* case (1992). This case contributed to the framework of equality rights jurisprudence by establishing that courts could, in some circumstances, "read in" new provisions to unconstitutionally underinclusive legislation. The CCP-funded parties urged the Court to adopt an expansive remedy of reading in, and the Court went some way to meeting their position. The program funded an assortment of other equality rights cases that applied this framework of interpretation. For example, it funded LEAF's interventions in the Charter's freedom of expression guarantees. These cases followed the substantive, "harm-based approach" that LEAF advocated, establishing that freedom of expression could be limited in order to protect vulnerable groups that might suffer adverse effects from certain kinds of expression (Hausegger 2000). Although some CCP-funded groups have lost in the Supreme Court, most have won.[18] In all, nine of the twenty-four equality rights cases the Supreme Court handed down between 1984 and 1993 had a party or intervener that was funded by the Court Challenges Program.[19] Overall, the program has funded groups that urged a substantive approach to equality rights, and in the cases it has funded the Supreme Court has generally followed a substantive equality approach.

Moreover, the CCP's impact comes in the context of wider government support for rights-oriented litigation in Canada. The federal and provincial governments provide important support to litigation through legal aid plans and the Department of Indian Affairs and Northern Development. As Morton and Knopff note, federal and provincial governments have encouraged rights-oriented litigation through law reform commissions, human rights commissions, and the law schools, many of whose faculty work for groups involved in litigation (Morton and Knopff 1991). Epp argues that these programs, along with the CCP, provided substantial, stable funding for rights advocacy and laid the groundwork for rights-oriented interest group litigation at the appellate level in Canada (Epp 1996).

The level of government support for rights litigation is pervasive; it is hard to isolate the impact of any one program. LEAF, for example, is the most frequent interest group intervener at the Supreme Court of Canada. This group emerged from a feminist mobilization for litigation in the wake of the adoption of the Charter of Rights. The federal government supported this mobilization in several ways. LEAF's original activists coalesced under the banner of the Charter of Rights Education Fund between 1982 and 1985. They received a grant from the Department of Justice to produce a comprehensive audit to see which federal and Ontario legislation did not comply with the substantive reading of the Charter's equality rights.[20] The plan to create LEAF was outlined in a report commissioned by the Canadian Advisory Council on the Status of Women, a federally funded organization (Atcheson, Eberts, and Symes 1984).[21] LEAF's founders were active in other government-funded feminist groups, and were, as Razack notes, all "well-versed in the arts of [government] grant applications . . . " (Razack 1991, 43). The feminist movement existed before LEAF did, and before the government-funded groups that were involved in creating LEAF. However, that movement could have taken many forms and pursued many kinds of political strategies. It opted to include litigation in its strategies. Government is not the reason it opted for litigation, but the federal government did play a role in the creation of LEAF and its litigation on behalf of the feminist movement in Canada.

CONCLUSION

The 1985 report *Equality for All* characterized section 15 cases as pitting "individuals on the one side and, generally speaking, government departments or agencies on the other side" (Canada 1985, 132). Yet, it is not easy to divide Charter litigants neatly into the categories of "public" and "private". The federal government encouraged interest group litigation through the Court Challenges Program. It sponsored litigation over language rights in order to undermine Bill 101 without confronting the Quebec government directly, and now sponsors equality rights cases as well.

As both Epp, and Morton and Knopff point out, the Charter is simply a document. Documents are not self-enforcing. To have full effect, the Charter needs interest groups ready to litigate. The Court Challenges Program was mobilizing OLMGs for litigation as the Charter was being debated. Later, it mobilized other groups to use the equality rights. In addition, the Charter itself was a government project. At a critical time during the patriation process, the Charter received important support from Secretary of State–funded interest groups.

This is not to say that interest group litigation, even in cases funded by the Court Challenges Program, is just a tool for the federal political objectives. As is the case with other Secretary of State programs, the federal government was as much a captive of the CCP as its purported clients. The CCP's efforts to build networks of groups were so successful that these networks were able to take advantage of the criticism the Mulroney government faced when it cancelled the Program and have the 1992 budget decision reversed. They then became more directly involved in the management of the renewed program. These groups are not merely pawns of the federal government. They have managed to harness access state funds to support their own activities in support of bilingualism and substantive equality rights.

Yet, the state's involvement is hard to square with the traditional view of judicial review and interest group litigation as a battle between the representatives of private individuals and governments. Society-centred and pluralist assumptions underlying the traditional view give judicial review and interest group litigation much of its normative justification. The argument here is not that government support for interest group litigation is necessarily problematic. Rather, it is that the contribution governments have made to the growth of interest group litigation in Canada forces us to reconsider the ideas underlying the traditional views of interest group litigation and judicial review. This conclusion is analytical, not ideological. The new judicial involvement in the policy process is sometimes a result of the state working through interest groups. The Court Challenges Program represents the embedded state at war with itself in court.

# POSTSCRIPT AND CONCLUSION

Since the early 1970s, the Supreme Court of Canada's role in Canada's political system has changed, and so has the Court's relationship with interest groups. The Court has, at times, struggled to find an appropriate place for interest groups in its work. Nevertheless, over the last thirty years interest groups have become much more frequent participants in the Court's work. This growth in interest group litigation has coincided with an impressive expansion of the Court's activism, an expansion that has generated little in the way of a political backlash. The Court's use of the disadvantaged group concept has allowed it to strike an implicit alliance with a loose coalition of interest groups. So long as the Court gives a privileged place to disadvantaged groups in both its treatment of interveners and its equality rights jurisprudence, they provide a ready justification for the Court's activist judicial review and claims to judicial supremacy.

The political disadvantage theory suggests that activist judicial review is at least a benign power if not a moral imperative. Activism in aid of disadvantaged groups gives judges a role in correcting what the theory sees as democracy's major structural defect: decisions are made by officials who must be responsive to political "majorities" and can therefore be insensitive to minorities. Courts face backlashes when they are seen to be engaged in illegitimate use of their powers. The political disadvantage theory has helped the Supreme Court of Canada head off the sorts of problems that the Judicial Committee of the Privy Council and the U.S. Supreme Court have encountered when they have engaged in activist judicial review. The Canadian Supreme Court has never explicitly founded its justification of its own role in the political disadvantage theory. When challenged, it still falls back on the legalistic defense of judicial supremacy. However, the Court's co-option of disadvantaged groups has helped it provide cover for its new role. The pluralist and society-centered premises of the political disadvantage theory—that interest group litigation emerges when groups of citizens band together to litigate when "normal" avenues of political action are blocked—constitute a powerful justification for judicial activism and supremacy.

However, the Supreme Court of Canada's role is not the benign or corrective one envisioned in the political disadvantage theory. Institutional self-interest is also at work. The Court uses the legitimacy supplied by interest groups that participate repeatedly in its work to expand its power. The concept of the disdavantaged group legitimates the Court's active use of the judicial review power and its claims to supremacy in the interpretation and enforcement of constitutional law. The Court is well on the road to establishing itself as a legislative, rather than a judicial, institution.

---

Recently, the Institute for Research on Public Policy published a monograph on interest group litigation in Canada by Gregory Hein (Hein 2000). Part of Hein's argument echoes the main tenets of the political disadvantage theory. While his analysis includes litigation by corporations, professionals, and conservative political interests, he pays particular attention to litigation by aboriginal Canadians, groups representing ethnic, religious, and linguistic minorities, women and the disabled, civil libertarians, and other "New Left" activists. These groups, he argues, have the greatest potential to influence public policy through litigation. He calls them "judicial democrats." Their legal arguments and political appeals, he writes, contain the "provocative idea" (5) that judicial review can enhance democracy. According to Hein's analysis, the judicial democrats find deficiencies in democratic politics.

These are the same deficiencies at the heart of the political disadvantage theory. Representative institutions do not fully represent the diversity of society. If courts do not enforce constitutional rights guarantees, governments may opt for policies that harm minorities. Their policies may not take into account the "weaker voices" in society. In Hein's view, the judicial democrats worry that while corporate interests get access to key government decision makers, other interests concerned about "public problems" (20) are often dismissed when they advance their concerns. Therefore, the judicial democrats argue, the courts must counter "grave threats" (21). Judges should listen to groups that lack political power, protect vulnerable minorities, and guard fundamental values (5). The judicial democrats believe litigation can make Canada's public institutions "more accessible, transparent and responsive" if the courts heed a "diverse range of interests, guard fundamental social values and protect disadvantaged minorities" (19). Hein's construction of the judicial democrat position has all the hallmarks of political disadvantage theory. Some groups are on the outside of the political process looking in, unable to get a fair hearing, or compete with better-organized and -positioned interests. Oppressive or at least unfavorable laws and policies burden these groups. They are forced to go to court to have their say. His use of the concept of the disadvantaged group and his analysis of the arguments against representative democracy draw heavily on the political disadvantage theory.

This book provides the material for a case against Hein's judicial democrats. The success that many of the "judicial democrats" have had in gaining government funding for their litigation belies the view that they are at a disadvantage in gaining access to political power or the resources of the state. While not all interest group litigation in Canada is aided by government action, the groups that have had government funding for their ongoing operations and their litigation projects—language groups, women's groups, ethnic groups, disabled groups—form the bulk of the "judicial democrat" coalition. If they have access to government funding, they cannot be terribly disadvantaged in access to political power. Rather, they are tied into networks of state power. They are able to secure funding from government departments and the Court Challenges Program.

This points to a deeper criticism of the political disadvantage theory and the concept of the disadvantaged group. The idea that interest group litigation emerges unaided from society when some segments of society find they cannot get a hearing in the political process is incomplete. In Canada, individuals do not simply band together to stop oppressive state action or to seek mandates for corrective state action. Judicial review in Canada is not typically a battle between private and state actors. Government action has played an important role in expanding interest group litigation, and mobilizing groups around litigation as a tactic for achieving their objectivs. The pluralist, bottom-up rhetoric that feeds the political disadvantage theory is a convenient ideology for group leaders who are quite well plugged into the state.

What is the future for the Canadian Supreme Court's relationship with interest groups? The Court has recently floated trial balloons about cutting back the number of interest group interveners it hears. In an interview in the spring of 2000, Justice Iacobucci questioned whether there are too many interveners, especially in criminal cases when "you have one person representing the accused and a battery of intervenors supporting the Crown, or vice versa. So they say you get into this kind of imbalance. I think we have to look at that." At the same time, he speculated that the Court needed interveners more in the early years of its Charter interpretation. "Looking back, those intervenors played a highly significant role. But it's now getting on to be 18 years or so later. Should we be looking at the question in different ways?"[1] Later that same spring, in an interview timed to coincide with the Court's 125th anniversary, Chief Justice McLachlin said it was "only just and fair" to allow intervenors in cases that will affect "not only the parties but a wide range of other people." Justice Bastarache suggested, in the same interview, that "we have lived with the Charter for 18 years. . . . There isn't the same need there was in 1982 to obtain help from intervenors."[2]

However, while the Court might cut back on the number of interveners it hears, it is unlikely to reverse the trend of widely involving more interest groups in its work. There has been considerable turnover on the Supreme Court bench since the late 1980s, but the Court's judges will remember the criticism leveled at their predecessors by interest groups and legal commentators when they tried to cut back on interventions. As long as the Court faces no pressures in the direction of limiting its links to interest groups, it is hard to imagine why the Court might risk another outburst of criticism by throttling back on intervention or the law of standing. The Court will only limit its accessibility to interest groups when it faces a price for not doing so. Such a countervailing force will only emerge if the Court overreaches with one of its decisions and provokes political backlash. So far, its work has not been seen as "overreaching" by many Canadians. The Court and its decisions remain extremely popular, particularly compared to the country's other institutions of government (Fletcher and Howe 2000).

# NOTES

## INTRODUCTION

1. F. L. Morton, "To bring judicial appointments out of the closet," *Global and Mail* Sep. 22, 1997.

## CHAPTER 1. THE POLITICAL DISADVANTAGE THEORY

1. His empirical findings here have recently faced an important challenge from Bohte, Flemming, and Wood 1995 and Flemming, Bohte, and Wood 1997.

2. Dennis Chong argues that during the 1950s and 1960s, southern blacks could participate in politics despite the barriers to voting by joining the direct action of the major civil rights groups. Because the NAACP provided limited opportunities for its members to participate in political action, it cut itself off from those blacks that wanted to invest their time and energy in a cause. "Instead of making a minimal financial contribution to the NAACP and thereby delegating responsibility to that organization to represent him in the struggle, an individual could instead get a hand in the action himself" (1991, 79). At the same time, Chong argues that the Supreme Court's civil rights decisions "boosted the morale of civil rights activists" after 1930 (170).

3. Scheppele and Walker (1991, 162) note that there is a high correlation between the size of a group's staff and its budget, making them almost interchangeable measures.

129

4. In practice, researchers usually impute a litigant's status rather than measure it directly. Bradley and Gardner assume business and trade groups, professional organizations, and corporations are upperdogs, while public interest, religious, racial, consumer, Native American, and labor organizations are underdogs. As a result, Bradley and Gardner's underdogs are for the most part O'Connor and Epstein's liberals, and the former's upperdogs are the latter's conservatives. Bradley and Gardner's broader categories let them classify labor unions as underdogs. O'Connor and Epstein exclude labor unions from their analysis, arguing that they have no consistent ideology.

5. The Court's only activist Bill of Rights decision prior to 1982 came in *Drybones* (1970). It invalidated part of the Indian Act that prohibited Indians from being intoxicated while off a reserve. Weiler (1974, 196–199) provides a good explanation of the limited impact of *Drybones*. The Court did not issue another activist Bill of Rights case again until 1985. That year, half the Court's judges ruled that Canada's system for determining refugee status was invalid under the Bill (*Singh* 1985).

6. *Tiny Township Roman Catholic Separate School Trustees* 1928.

7. There is one main difference between the American and Canadian versions of the political disadvantage theory. The Canadian version has downplayed the concept of "discrete and insular minorities." In this way, women can fit into the list of disadvantaged groups. In *Andrews*, Wilson was careful to note that "the range of discrete and insular minorities has changed and will continue to change with changing political and social circumstances" (1989, 33). In 1938, Justice Stone had been concerned with religious, national, and racial minorities. In 1982, the Charter's framers extended the reach of the concept to include many other groups, including women. In *Turpin*, Wilson "hasten[ed] to add" that the concept was "merely one of the analytical tools which are of assistance" in deciding whether any particular interest "is the kind of interest s. 15 of the *Charter* is designed to protect" (1989, 1333).

## Chapter 2. Interveners at the Supreme Court of Canada

1. Some courts have the power to hear third parties "expressly conferred by statute or by court rules." In such instances, the third parties are called interveners. In other courts, the power to hear third parties "is based on the courts' inherent authority" (Gibson 1986, 271). In these

instances, they are called amici curiae. Since the Canadian Supreme Court has long allowed for third parties in its rules, it calls them "interveners."

2. See Friedland 1984, 98 and 99 for examples of interest group participation in early reference cases.

3. Muldoon says there are instances "as far back as 1945 where persons or organizations have been permitted to intervene specifically to argue a particular position," referring to *re: Wren* (1989, 119).

4. The Supreme Court of Canada, for example, provided for interveners in its first set of rules, in 1878.

5. The leading sources are Caldeira and Wright 1990; O'Connor and Epstein 1981–1982; Puro 1971; Barker 1967; Hakman 1966; Krislov 1963; and Vose 1959 and 1958.

6. The Department of Justice pursued the first campaign of planned amicus activity after it was created in 1871. Charles Bonaparte, U.S. Attorney General from 1906 to 1909, used the amicus procedure to promote the rights of blacks and to defend the legislation of the federal government. State law officers began to appear as friends of the U.S. Supreme Court in the 1880s (Barker 1967, 1018).

7. It had already appeared in a few lower court cases. See Kellogg 1967, 57–65; and Kluger 1976, 101.

8. O'Connor and Epstein's figures for the years before 1970 do not match Puro's. It is impossible from their article to determine how their methodology differs from his. Nonetheless, the figures are similar, if not exactly comparable.

9. The creation of the Federal Court of Appeal in 1971 also relieved the Supreme Court of the need to hear routine appeals from the Exchequer/Federal Court (Russell 1987, 311).

10. Supreme Court case file *R v Valente* (1985).

11. Manfredi conceives of constitutional amendment and constitutional litigation as two levels of a single, nested game (Tsebelis 1990). Political authorities set out "first order rules" for constitutional interpretation in the texts of constitutions and constitutional amendments. These first order rules are then elaborated in the courts or elsewhere. Within the constraints of first order rules judicial precedents set "second order rules" for constitutional interpretation. Second order rules in turn may become roadblocks to the development of new first order rules in constitutional amendments. See Manfredi 1992, 1993b.

12. Romanow, Whyte, and Leeson 1984 is the comprehensive account of the intergovernmental process leading up to patriation, but it tends to understate the influence of interest groups and the activities of the Special Joint Committee. A better account of these actors can be found in Williams 1985 and Knopff and Morton 1992. The feminists' account of the debates is found in Kome 1983. Much of my account is drawn from Hos'ek 1983 and Razack 1991.

13. The NAACP, the NAACP Legal Defense and Education Fund, the ACLU, the ACLU Women's Rights Project, the National Organization of Women's Legal Defense and Education Fund, the Women's Equity Action League, the Women's Legal Defense Fund, the Women's Law Fund, the Women's Law Project in Philadelphia, Equal Rights Advocates in San Francisco, the National Women's Law Centre, the Centre for Constitutional Rights, the League of Women's Voters Education Fund, the National Center for Women and Family Law and the National Employment Law Project are all surveyed in the report (Atcheson, Eberts, and Symes 1984, 114–144).

14. Kluger 1977; Council of Public Interest Law 1976; Pinzler et al. 1982; Cowan 1976; Berger 1980; and Vose 1955 to name only a few sources.

15. The CACSW report recommended that a legal fund should focus more on sponsoring test cases than intervening. "It is becoming increasingly difficult for non-parties to intervene in ordinary court proceedings and it is difficult to predict how receptive courts will be to such interventions in Charter cases" (Atcheson, Eberts, and Symes, 1984, 167). As outlined below, these concerns about the hostility of the Supreme Court to interveners would soon become irrelevant.

16. Section 1 states that the rights and freedoms set out in the Charter are guaranteed, "subject only to such reasonable limits prescribed by law as can be demonstrably justified in a free and democratic society."

17. SOR/82-74 11 January, 1983. *Canada Gazette*, Part II, vol. 117, no. 2, p. 380.

18. Rule 60 had read as follows:

(1) Any person interested in an appeal may, by leave of the Court or a Judge, intervene therein upon such terms and conditions and with such rights and privileges as the Court or Judge

may determine. (2) The costs of such intervention shall be paid by such party or parties as the Supreme Court shall order.

19. *R v Ogg-Moss* [1984], 2 S.C.R. 171. Ritchie, for Dickson, Estey, McIntyre, and Chouinard.

20. SOR/83-930, 5 December, 1983. *Canada Gazette*, Part II, vol. 117, no. 23, p. 4363.

21. There was also a pained reaction in the academic literature. Although it is difficult to separate the academic commentary from the interest group advocacy on this point, the literature published in academic sources is more fully canvassed in chapter 3.

22. Stephen Bindman, "Door Open: Supreme Court lets groups intervene in cases," *Ottawa Citizen*, March 9, 1991, B8.

23. The CCLA submitted the same brief that Borovoy had submitted to the Court itself. LEAF's submission is summarized in Eberts, Brodsky, and Joanis 1987. The BC Civil Liberties Association presented an abridged version of Bryden 1987 (see Bryden 1989). PIAC lost its copy of its submission when it closed its Toronto office. Bryden also claims that the Canadian Labour Congress submitted a brief, but they have no record of such a submission.

24. SOR/ 87-792, 22 May, 1987. *Canada Gazette*, Part II, vol. 121, no. 12, p. 2153.

25. LEAF has a following that charts its success rates in leave to intervene applications. Steel and Smith use the possessive "our" to describe LEAF's interest in the 1988 case of *Klachefsky v Brown* (1989, 69). Steel has served as a member of LEAF's Legal Committee. Koch also singles out LEAF's success rate in his analysis (1990, 163).

26. Welch (1985, 223) and Swan (1987, 43) both make this criticism.

27. Welch writes that since Charter cases involve the interests of governments and individuals, representatives of both governments and of the "individual writ large" (i.e., interest groups) should be allowed to appear before the courts (Welch 1985, 225). "[T]he willingness of courts to listen to intervenors is a reflection of the values that judges attach to people" (Bryden 1987, 509).

28. The table might therefore underrate cases that were not heard on their merits until 2000. Interveners might have been added to those cases in early 2000.

## Chapter 3. Interest Group Litigation and Judicial Supremacy

1. S. 52(1) The Constitution of Canada is the supreme law of Canada, and any law that is inconsistent with the provisions of the Constitution is, to the extent of the inconsistency, of no force or effect.

2. S. 24. (1) Anyone whose rights or freedoms, as guaranteed by this Charter, have been infringed or denied may apply to a court of competent jurisdiction to obtain such remedy as the court considers appropriate and just in the circumstances.

3. Note that the legalistic argument leads to lax rules of standing, even as it supports only a restricted right to intervention. Lax rules of standing ensure that any dispute over the interpretation of the constitution can work its way into court. Anyone should be able to challenge the constitutionality of a government action, regardless of whether they meet the traditional rules of standing. But once a lawsuit begins, interest groups can intervene only if they are needed to give a full hearing to the legal issues at stake.

4. As it turns out, nongovernment interveners in Canada actually do a poor job of bringing scientific and other similar forms of extrinsic evidence before the Supreme Court (Morton and Brodie 1993). It is also not clear that the courts can make use of Brandeis brief information. Judges' ability to make use of social sciences or other forms of extrinsic evidence is an issue not a fact, as the *Askov* 1990 and *Morin* 1992 cases demonstrate (Baar 1993; see also Pepall 1996).

5. He cited the Court's decision in the 1969 *Norcan* case to support the view that "any" interest in a case is sufficient grounds for an intervention. Justice Pigeon had stated in *Norcan* that "any interest" was a sufficient basis for an intervention, but both Bryden (1987, 501) and Muldoon (1989, 182) argue that the context of Pigeon's remarks makes it clear that he meant any *financial* interest was sufficient. *Norcan* was a strictly private law case in which one party had fled the country by the time the case arrived at the Supreme Court. Bondsmen for the party applied to intervene at the Supreme Court. Allowing them to intervene let the Court resolve a long-standing private dispute. The decision therefore probably did not stand for the proposition that *any* interest in the precedent to be established in a case was sufficient to become an intervener.

6. Muldoon (1989, 153) and Koch (1990, 155) make similar statements.

7. An application to re-hear the case was refused by LaForest, L'Heureux-Dubé, Sopinka, Gonthier, Cory, and McLachlin on October 3, 1991. See 1991 SCN, Vol. 7, No. 12 at page 167. The Court (L'Heureux-Dubé, Gonthier and McLachlin) later denied leave to appeal in another NCC-sponsored test case, *Janzen v A-G British Columbia et al.*, on November 3, 1994. This case asked the Court to reconsider its position that parties might be liable for the costs of interveners.

8. See also Manfredi 1991; Hiebert 1989–1990.

## CHAPTER 4. THE MARKET FOR SECTION 15 STATUS

1. The original October 1980 text of section 15 (1) read:

Everyone has the right to equality before the law and to the equal protection of the law without discrimination because of race, national or ethnic origin, colour, religion, age or sex.

The revised wording was deliberately designed to override some Supreme Court of Canada equality rights decisions under the 1960 Bill of Rights (see Atcheson, Eberts, and Symes 1984).

2. Knopff 1989, 28. Again, the best account of feminist efforts to redraft the Charter is Razack 1991, 32.

3. Wilson made this comment originally in her concurring opinion in *Andrews* (1989, 152). She repeated it for a unanimous Court in *Turpin* (1989, 1331).

4. *Andrews* (1989).

5. *Haig and Birch* (1992), *Egan* (1995), *Vriend* (1998).

6. See *Walker and Robertson* (1992). Walker and Robertson's section 15 claim was denied at trial (337–339), but they won the case on other grounds. The trial decision was reversed on appeal (*Walker and Robertson* [1993] [PEI CA]; *Walker and Robertson* [1995] [SCC]). I thank Mary Eberts, counsel for Walker and Robertson, for her help in locating the documents relating to this case.

7. The classic treatment is Luce and Raiffa 1957. Axelrod 1984 extends the analysis to n-persons.

8. This outcome is the equilibrium in a one-time situation. In an infinite number of iterations, Keep Quiet might become the equilibrium. See Axelrod 1984, 12–24.

9. Ostrom 1990 provides a fuller treatment of these "common pool resource" situations.

10. Schelling does not speak of a v-point. The term is from Chong 1991, 110.

11. See the annual reports of the Court Challenges Program's equality rights panel (Court Challenges Program Equality Rights Panel 1988, 1989, 1990).

12. *Walker and Robertson* (1992).

13. Morton 1993; Razack 1991, 37. Academic legal commentary has a similar legitimizing influence in France. See Stone 1992, 93–104.

14. On the role of the equality rights provision in the policy-making process, see Manfredi 1993a, chapter 5.

15. Similarly, it is interesting to note that federal governments and the courts often ignored the rights of francophones outside Quebec until the concept of Official Language Minority Groups was coined and extended to Quebec anglophones.

16. Brodsky and Day (1989) express the fear that section 15 status might be extended to some inappropriate groups.

17. *Fair Employment Practices Act*, S.O. 1951, c. 24, and *Fair Accommodation Practices Act*, S.O. 1954, c. 28. See Howe 1991, 791.

18. In other words, the Code now covers instances of disparate impact. Minimum height and weight requirements for jobs were not impugned by the original Code since they discriminated only against short or underweight people, but they disproportionately exclude women from jobs so are now subject to review under the Code. See Knopff 1989, 45–59.

19. The 1981 Code also generally replaced "nationality" with "ethnic origin" as a ground of discrimination. Discrimination on the basis of record of offenses was outlawed in employment, but not in the provision of services, goods, and facilities. Discrimination on the basis of age was limited to people of eighteen years or more, and less than sixty-five in the case of employment.

20. *Equality Rights Statute Law*, S.O. 1986, c. 64, s. 18.

21. A 1986 project to make all Ontario laws comply with section 15 of the Charter added sexual orientation to the Code. The C for sexual orientation was probably reduced because of the general revision project.

22. *Pay Equity Act*, R.S.O. 1990, c. P.7.

CHAPTER 5. POLITICAL DISADVANTAGE AND STATE ACTION

1. Pal (1993, 33–34) hints at there being two stages in Cairns's treatment of the state, but does not draw the distinction as sharply as I have here.

2. Part of this history is taken from Brodie 1992.

3. Trudeau 1968. See also Mandel 1989, 90–96.

4. See Karwacki 1994, 19–23, and "Won't test Quebec law, Ottawa says," *Globe and Mail*, Oct. 7, 1977, 1.

5. In the committee's words, "Many of the witnesses appearing before the Committee emphasized the need for some form of funding by the federal government of section 15 litigation." It specifically lists the Canadian Ethno-Cultural Council, the Coalition of Provincial Organizations of the Handicapped, the Canadian Bar Association (CBA), the National Action Committee on the Status of Women, and LEAF (Canada 1985). All of these organizations except the CBA were receiving funds from Secretary of State citizenship programs at the time.

6. Author's interview with John Crosbie, January 30, 1999, Ottawa.

7. The CCSD was chosen "because of its previous interest in equality rights, because it had provided informal consultative advice to the voluntary sector and to government regarding the Charter, and because it had committed itself to a continuing process of sharing information and experience" (Canada 1989, 7).

8. Bureau of Management Consulting 1989: 29. Public Information included all the promotional activities of the program, including the costs of program-sponsored conferences and publishing.

9. According to the program's Annual Reports and records released under the *Access to Information Act*.

10. The Human Rights Research and Education Centre received $294,476 from the Secretary of State between 1985/1986 and 1987/1988. Canada, *Public Accounts of Canada*, 1985/1986 to 1987/1988.

11. These quotations are taken from "Ottawa ends aid for Charter cases," *Globe and Mail*, Feb. 28, 1992, and "Language minorities lament loss of aid for Charter challenges," *Globe and Mail*, Feb. 29, 1992.

12. "Canada gaining hypocrite tag, human-rights commission says," *Globe and Mail*, March 27, 1992.

13. "Rock pledges program's revival," *Globe and Mail*, Nov. 15, 1993.

14. These number come from CCP case files released under the *Access to Information Act*. The files that have been released do not indicate how

much funding was committed to eleven of those interventions. If the program committed its maximum permissible grant of $35,000 to these interventions (and if LEAF received only one $35,000 commitment for its interventions in the companion cases *Taylor, Andrews,* and *Keegstra*), then the CCP's total support to these thirty-five interventions would total $650,850.

15. *Andrews* 1989, Court Challenges Program, Equality Rights Panel 1987–1988, 18–19.

16. Three challenges at the county court and the Manitoba Court of Appeal did overturn the 1890 Act, but these decisions were ignored at the time. See Wiseman 1992, 703.

17. On the distinction between "substantive" and "formal" approaches to equality, see Manfredi 1993a, 121–127.

18. LEAF lost its defense of the "rape shield" law in *Seaboyer* (1991). The Court refused to back the Canadian Council of Churches in its quest to expand the law of public interest standing, although Canada's law of standing was already quite wide (*Canadian Council of Churches* 1992). Also, Mossop lost his bid to have a denial of same sex partner bereavement leave considered discrimination based on family status under the Canadian Human Rights Act, but the Supreme Court has delivered a number of victories to gay rights groups since then and essentially undone *Mossop*'s impact (1993).

19. The count of twenty-four cases considers *Harrison v University of British Columbia* (1990), *Stoffman v Vancouver General Hospital* (1990), *McKinney v University of Guelph* (1990), and *Douglas/Kwantlen Faculty Association v. Douglas College* (1990), as one case. It also considers *R v S(G)* (1990), *R v P(J)* (1990), and *R v T(A)* (1990) as one case.

20. Canada 1984, 51. See also Razack 1991, 38.

21. This report was commissioned in response to suggestions first raised at a CACSW conference in the spring of 1981 (Atcheson, Eberts, and Symes 1984, 2–3).

## POSTCRIPT AND CONCLUSION

1. Kirk Makin, "Intevenors: how many are too many?" *Globe and Mail,* March 10, 2000.

2. Luiza Chwialkowska, "Rein in lobby groups, senior judges suggest," *National Post,* April 6, 2000.

# REFERENCES

## CASES

*Ah How*, (1904) 193 US 65.

*Andrews v R.*, (1990) 3 S.C.R. 870.

*Andrews v Law Society of British Columbia*, (1989) 1 S.C.R. 143.

*R. v Askov*, (1990) 2 S.C.R. 1199.

*Baker v Carr*, (1962) 369 U.S. 186.

*Barrett v City of Winnipeg*, (1892) A.C. 445.

*Barrett v City of Winnipeg*, (1891) S.C.R. 374.

*Bilodeau v Attorney-General of Manitoba*, (1986) 1 S.C.R. 449.

*A-G Que. v Blaikie*, (1981) 1 S.C.R. 312.

*A-G Que. v Blaikie*, (1979) 2 S.C.R. 1016.

*Blainey v A-G Ontario*, (1986) 54 O.R. (2nd) 513.

*Bliss v A-G Canada*, (1979) 1 S.C.R. 183.

*Boland v MPVR*, (1993) D.T.C. 1553.

*Minister of Justice of Canada v Borowski*, (1981) 2 S.C.R. 575.

*British Columbia Government Employees' Union v A-G British Columbia*, (1988) 53 D.L.R. (4th) 1 (Supreme Court of Canada).

*Brown v Board of Education,* (1954) 3347 U.S. 483.

*R v Butler,* (1992) 1 S.C.R. 452.

*Canadian Council of Churches v Canada (Minister of Employment and Immigration,* (1992) 1 S.C.R. 236.

*Canadian Newspapers Co v A-G of Canada,* (1988) 2 S.C.R. 122.

*United States v Carolene Products Co,* (1938) 304 U.S. 144.

*Delgamuukw v British Columbia,* (1997) 3 S.C.R. 1010.

*Douglas/Kwantlen Faculty Association v Douglas College,* (1990) 3 S.C.R. 570.

*R v Drybones,* (1970) S.C.R. 282.

*R v Edwards Books and Art,* (1986) 2 S.C.R. 713.

*Egan v Canada,* (1995) 2 S.C.R. 513.

*R v Finta,* (1993) 1 S.C.R. 1138.

*Ford v Quebec (AG),* (1988) 2 S.C.R. 712.

*Furman v Georgia,* (1972) 408 U. S. 238.

*Griswold v Connecticut,* (1965) 387 U.S. 479.

*Guinn v US,* (1915) 238 U.S. 347.

*Haig and Birch v Canada,* (1992) 95 D.L.R. (4th ) 1.

*Harper v Harper,* (1980) 1 S.C.R. 2.

*Harrison v University of British Columbia,* (1990) 3 S.C.R. 451.

*Janzen v A-G British Columbia, S.C.B.* (November 4, 1994).

*R v Keegstra,* (1990) 3 S.C.R. 697.

*Klachefsky v Brown,* (1988) 1 W.W.R. 755.

*A-G Canada v Lavell, Isaac et al. v Bedard,* (1974) S.C.R. 1349.

*Lavigne v Ontario Public Service Employees Union,* (1991) 2 S.C.R. 211.

*Law v Canada (Minister of Employment and Immigration),* (1999) 1 S.C.R. 497.

*M(K) v M(H),* (1992) 3 S.C.R. 3.

*M v H,* [1999] 2 S.C.R. 3

*MacDonald v City of Montreal,* (1986) 1 S.C.R. 460.

*Mahe v Alberta,* (1990) 1 S.C.R. 342.

*Mapp v Ohio,* (1961) 367 U. S. 643.

*Marbury v Madison,* (1803) 1 Cranch 137.

*R v Marshall,* [1999] 3 S.C.R. 533

*McKinney v University of Guelph,* (1990) 3 S.C.R. 229.

*Nova Scotia Bd. of Censors v. McNeil,* (1976) 2 S.C.R. 265.

*R v Mercure,* (1988) 1 S.C.R. 234.

*Miranda v Arizona,* (1966) 384 U.S. 430.

*Miron v Trudel,* (1995) 2 S.C.R. 418.

*R v Morgentaler,* (1976) 1 S.C.R. 616.

*R v Morgentaler, Smoling and Scott,* (1993) 1 S.C.R. 462.

*R v Morin,* (1992)

*Canada (Attorney General) v Mossop,* (1993) 1 S.C.R.

*New Brunswick Broadcasting v Nova Scotia (Speaker of the Legislative Assembly),* (1993) 1 S.C.R. 319.

*Norberg v Wynrib,* (1992) 2 S.C.R. 224.

*Norcan v Lebrock,* (1969) S.C.R. 665.

*Nova Scotia Board of Censors v McNeil,* (1976) 2 S.C.R. 265.

*Nova Scotia Pharmaceuticals Society v The Queen,* (1992) 2 S.C.R. 606.

*R v Ogg-Moss,* (1984) 2 S.C.R. 171.

*Operation Dismantle v The Queen,* (1985) 1 S.C.R. 441.

*R v P(J),* (1990) 2 S.C.R. 300.

*Poe v Ullman,* (1961) 367 U.S. 497.

*Reference re: Bill 30 (Ont. Separate School Funding),* (1987) 1 S.C.R. 1148.

*Reference re: Firearms,* (2000) 1 S.C.R. 783.

*Reference re: Manitoba Language Rights,* (1992) 1 S.C.R. 212.

*Reference re: Manitoba Language Rights,* (1985) 1 S.C.R. 721.

*Reference re: Public Schools Act (Manitoba),* (1993) 1 S.C.R. 839.

*Reference re: Motor Vehicles Act , 1985 (British Columbia)*, (1985) 24 D.L.R. (4th) 536.

*Reference re: Workers' Compensation Act, 1983(Newfoundland)*, (1989) 2 S.C.R. 335 (Coté application for leave to intervene).

*Robertson and Rosetanni v The Queen*, (1963) S.C.R. 651.

*R v S(G)*, (1990) 2 S.C.R. 294.

*Schacter v Canada*, (1992) 2 S.C.R. 679.

*Seaboyer v The Queen*, (1991) 2 S.C.R. 577.

*R v Sheldon S*, (1990) 2 S.C.R. 254.

*Sinclair v Quebec (Attorney-General)*, (1992) 1 S.C.R. 579.

*Singh et al v Minister of Employment and Immigration*, (1985) 1 S.C.R. 177.

*Law Society of Upper Canada v Skapinker*, (1984) 1 S.C.R. 357.

*Smith v A.-G. Ontario*, (1924) S.C.R. 331.

*Société des Acadiens v Association des Parents*, (1986) 1 S.C.R. 549.

*Sparrow v The Queen*, (1990) 1 S.C.R. 1075.

*Stoffman v Vancouver General Hospital*, (1990) 3 S.C.R. 483.

*R v Swain*, (1991) 1 S.C.R. 933.

*Symes v Canada*, (1993) 4 S.C.R. 695.

*R v T(a)*, (1990) 2 S.C.R. 304.

*Canada (Human Rights Commission) v Taylor*, (1990) 3 S.C.R. 66.

*Tétrault-Gadoury v Canada*, (1991) 2 S.C.R. 22.

*Thorson v A-G Canada*, (1975) 1 S.C.R. 138.

*Tiny Township Roman Catholic Separate School Trustees v The King*, (1928) A.C. 363.

*R v Turpin*, (1989) 1 S.C.R. 1296.

*Valente v The Queen*, (1985) 2 S.C.R. 673.

*Vriend v Alberta*, (1998) 1 S.C.R. 493.

*Walker and Robertson v PEI*, (1995) 2 S.C.R. 407 (S.C.C.).

*Walker and Robertson v PEI*, (1993) 107 D.L.R. (4th) 69 (P.E.I. Supreme Court, Appeal Division).

*Walker and Robertson v PEI*, (1992) 101 Nfld. & P. E. I. R. 303.

*Weatherall v Canada*, (1993) 2 S.C.R. 872.

*re: Drummond Wren*, (1945) 4 D.L.R. 674.

*R v Zundel*, (1992) 2 S.C.R. 731.


OTHER REFERENCES


Atcheson, Beth, Mary Eberts, and Beth Symes, with Jennifer Stoddart. 1984. *Women and Legal Action: Precedents, Resources, and Strategies for the Future*. Ottawa: Canadian Advisory Council on the Status of Women.

Axelrod, Robert. 1984. *The Evolution of Cooperation*. New York: Basic Books.

Baar, Carl. 1993. "Criminal Court Delay and the Charter: The Use and Misuse of Social Facts in Judicial Policy Making," *Canadian Bar Review* 72: 304–336.

Bakan, Joel. 1997. *Just Words: Constitutional Rights and Social Wrongs*. Toronto : University of Toronto Press

Barker, Lucius. 1967. "Third Parties in Litigation: A Systematic View of the Judicial Function," *Journal of Politics* 24: 41–69.

Bentley, Arthur B. 1967 [1908]. *The Process of Government*. Cambridge, MA: Belknap Press.

Berger, Margaret A. 1980. *Litigation on Behalf of Women: A Review for the Ford Foundation*. New York: Ford Foundation.

Berger, Thomas. 1982. *Fragile Freedoms: Human Rights and Dissent in Canada*. Toronto: Clarke, Irwin.

Bogart, W. A. 1994. *Courts and Country*. Toronto: Oxford.

Bohte, John, Roy B. Flemming, and B. Dan Wood. 1995. "The Supreme Court, the Media, and Legal Change: A Reassessment of Rosenberg's *Hollow Hope*." Presented at the Annual Meeting of the American Political Science Association, Chicago.

Borovoy, A. Alan. 1986. "Letter to the Honourable Ray Hnatyshyn, QC., Federal Minister of Justice." Dated December 23, 1986. Toronto: Canadian Civil Liberties Association.

———. 1984. Submissions to [the] Supreme Court of Canada Re: Interventions in Public Interest Litigation From Canadian Civil Liberties

Association per A. Alan Borovoy (General Counsel). Toronto: Canadian Civil Liberties Association, July 24.

Botting, Gary. 1993. *Fundamental freedoms and Jehovah's Witnesses.* Calgary: University of Calgary Press.

Bradley, Robert C., and Paul Gardner. 1985. "Underdogs, Upperdogs, and the Use of the Amicus Curiae Brief," *Justice System Journal* 19: 78–96.

Brodie, Ian. 1996. "The Market for Political Status," *Comparative Politics* 28: 253–271.

————, and Neil Nevitte. 1993a. "Evaluating the Citizens' Constitution Theory," *Canadian Journal of Political Science* 26: 235–259.

————, and Neil Nevitte. 1993b. "Clarifying Differences: A Rejoinder to Alan Cairns," *Canadian Journal of Political Science* 26: 269–272.

————. 1993c. "Interest Groups in Court: Beyond `Beyond the Political Disadvantage Theory'." Occasional Papers, Research Unit for Socio-Legal Studies, University of Calgary.

————. 1993d. "Competition for Charter Equality Rights Status: The Rational Choice Dynamic." Presented to the annual meetings of the Canadian Political Science Association, June, Carleton University, Ottawa.

————. 1993e. "Competition for Equality Rights Status in the Canadian Charter of Rights and Freedoms." Prepared for the annual meetings of the Law and Society Association, Chicago.

————. 1993f. "Competition for Equality Rights Status: A Rational Choice Model and a Test." Presented to the Biennial Meetings of the Association for Canadian Studies in the United States, November, New Orleans.

————. 1992. "The Court Challenges Program." In *Law, Politics, and the Judicial Process in Canada,* ed. F. L. Morton. Calgary: University of Calgary Press.

Brodsky, Gwen, and Shelagh Day. 1989. *Canadian Charter Equality Rights for Women: One Step Forward or Two Steps Back?* Ottawa: Canadian Advisory Council on the Status of Women.

Bruer, Patrick. 1988. "Amicus Curiae and Supreme Court Litigation." Presented at the Annual meeting of the Law and Society Association, Vail, Colorado.

Bryden, Philip L. 1989. "Public Interest Intervention Before the Courts." In *Liberties*, ed. John Russel. Vancouver: New Star Books.

———. 1987. "Public Interest Intervention in the Courts," *Canadian Bar Review* 66: 490–528.

Bureau of Management Consulting. 1989. "Court Challenges Program Administrative Review—Project No. 4–7645." Ottawa: Department of Supply and Services, October.

Bushnell, S. I. 1982. "Leave to Appeal Applications to the Supreme Court of Canada: A Matter of Public Importance." *Supreme Court Law Review* 3: 481–558.

Cairns, Alan C. 1988. "Citizens (Outsiders) and Government (Insiders) in Constitution-Making: The Case of Meech Lake," *Canadian Public Policy* 14: S 121–145.

———. 1985. "The Embedded State." In *Perspectives on the State*, ed. Keith Banting. Toronto: University of Toronto Press.

———. 1979. "The Other Crisis of Canadian Federalism," *Canadian Public Administration* 22: 175–195, reprinted in *Constitution, Government, and Society in Canada*, ed. Douglas E. Williams. Toronto: McClelland and Stewart, 1988.

———. 1977. "The Governments and Societies of Canadian Federalism," *Canadian Journal of Political Science* 7: 192–234, reprinted in *Constitution, Government, and Society in Canada*, ed. Douglas E. Williams. Toronto: McClelland and Stewart, 1988.

Caldeira, Gregory A., and John R. Wright. 1990. "Amici Curiae Before the Supreme Court: Who Participates, When, and How Much?" *Journal of Politics* 52: 782–806.

Canada. 1992. *Paying Too Dearly*. Ottawa: House of Commons.

Canada. 1989. *Court Challenges Program: First Report of the Standing Committee on Human Rights and the Status of Disabled Persons.* Ottawa: House of Commons.

Canada. 1985. *Equality for All*. Ottawa: House of Commons.

Canada. 1984. *Department of Justice, Annual Report, 1983–84.* Ottawa: Minister of Supply and Services.

Canadian Bar Association. 1991. *Public Interest Intervention Policy*. Ottawa.

Canadian Human Rights Commission. 1993. *Annual Report 1992*. Ottawa: Canadian Human Rights Commission.

Chester, S. 1983. "Holy Joe and the Most Vexed Question—Standing to Sue and the Supreme Court of Canada," *Supreme Court Law Review* 5: 289–308.

Chong, Dennis. 1991. *Collection Action and the Civil Rights Movement.* Chicago: University of Chicago Press.

Clark, Samuel. 1995. *State and Status: The Rise of the State and Aristocratic Power in Western Europe.* Montreal: McGill-Queen's Press.

Commissioner of Official Languages. 1993. *Annual Report 1992.* Ottawa: Commissioner of Official Languages.

Cortner, Richard C. 1968. "Strategies and Tactics of Litigants in Constitutional Cases," *Journal of Public Law* 17: 287–307.

Council of Public Interest Law. 1976. *Balancing the Scales of Justice: Financing Public Interest Law in America.* Washington, DC: Council of Public Interest Law.

Court Challenges Program, Equality Rights Panel. 1989–1990. *Annual Report.* Toronto: Canadian Council on Social Development.

Court Challenges Program, Language Rights Panel. 1989–1990. *Annual Report.* Toronto: Canadian Council on Social Development.

Court Challenges Program, Equality Rights Panel. 1988–1989. *Annual Report.* Toronto: Canadian Council on Social Development.

Court Challenges Program, Equality Rights Panel. 1987–1988. *Annual Report.* Toronto: Canadian Council on Social Development.

Cowan, Ruth B. 1976. "Women's Rights Through Litigation: An Examination of the American Civil Liberties Union Women's Rights Project, 1971–1976," *Columbia Human Rights Review* 8: 373–412.

Crane, B. A. 1986. "C.B.A. Supreme Court of Canada Liaison Committee." Report dated November 25, 1986. Ottawa: Canadian Bar Association.

———, and H. Brown. 1995. *Supreme Court of Canada Practice 1996.* Scarborough: Carswell.

Dickens, Bernard M. 1977. "A Canadian Development: Non Party Intervention," *Modern Law Review* 40: 666–676.

Ely, John Hart. 1980. *Democracy and Distrust: Judicial Review and Representative* Government. Cambridge, MA: Harvard University Press.

Epp, Charles R. 1996. "Do Bills of Rights Matter? The Canadian Charter of Rights and Freedoms," *American Political Science Review* 90: 765–779.

Epstein, Lee, Jeffrey A. Segal, Harold J. Spaeth, and Thomas G. Walker. 1996. *The Supreme Court Compendium: Decisions and Developments.* Washington, DC: Congressional Quarterly Press.

Epstein, Lee, and C. K. Rowland. 1991. "Debunking the Myth of Interest Group Invincibility in the Courts," *American Political Science Review* 85: 205–217.

Evans, J. M. 1981. "Standing to Challenge Unlawful Tax Expenditures," *Canadian Taxation:* 17–28.

Flanagan, Thomas. 1985. "The Manufacture of Minorities." In *Minorities and the Canadian State*, ed. Neil Nevitte and Allan Kornberg. Oakville: Mosaic.

Flemming, Roy B., John Bohte, and B. Dan Wood. 1997. "One Voice Among Many: The Supreme Court's Influence on Attentiveness to Issues in the United States, 1947–1990," *American Journal of Political Science* (forthcoming).

Fletcher, Joseph F., and Paul Howe. 2000. "Canadian Attitudes Towards the Charter and the Courts in Comparative Perspective," *Choices* 6: 4–29.

Friedland, Martin L. 1984. *A Century of Criminal Justice: Perspectives on the Development of Canadian Law.* Toronto: Carswell.

Galanter, Marc. 1974–1975. "Why the 'Haves' Come Out Ahead: Speculation on the Limits of Legal Change," *Law & Society Review* 9: 95–160.

Gibson, Dale. 1986. *The Law of the Charter: General Principles.* Toronto: Carswell.

Goreham, Richard. 1992. *Language Rights and the Court Challenges Program: A Review of Its Accomplishments and Impact of Its Abolition.* Ottawa: Commissioner of Official Languages.

Hakman, Nathan. 1966. "Lobbying the Supreme Court: A Critical Analysis of Political Science 'Folklore'," *Fordham Law Review* 35: 15–50.

Hausegger Lori Joanne. 2000. "The impact of interest groups on judicial decision making: A comparison of women's groups in the U.S. and Canada." Ph.D. Dissertation, Ohio State University.

———. 1994. "The Effectiveness of Interest Group Litigation: An Assessment of LEAF's Participation in Supreme Court Cases." M.A. Thesis, University of Calgary.

Heard, Andrew. 1991. "The Charter in the Supreme Court of Canada: The Importance of Which Judges Hear an Appeal," *Canadian Journal of Political Science* 24: 289–307.

Hein, Gregory. 2000. "Interest Group Litigation and Canadian Democracy," *Choices* 6: 1–31.

Hiebert, Janet. 1989–1990. "Fair Elections and Freedom of Expression under the Charter," *Journal of Canadian Studies* 24: 72–86.

Hogg, Peter W. 1999. *Constitutional Law of Canada, 1999 Student Edition*. Toronto: Carswell.

Horowitz, Donald L. 1977. *The Courts and Social Policy*. Washington, DC: The Brookings Institution.

Hosek, Chaviva. 1983. "Women in the Constitutional Process." In *And No One Cheered: Federalism, Democracy, and the Constitution Act*, ed. Keith Banting and Richard Simeon. Toronto: Methuen.

Howe, R. Brian. 1991. "The Evolution of Human Rights Policy in Ontario,"*Canadian Journal of Political Science* 24: 783–802.

Hutchinson, Allan. 1995. *Waiting for Coraf*. Toronto: University of Toronto Press.

Kaplan, William. 1989. *State and Salvation: The Jehovah's Witnesses and Their Fight for Civil Rights*. Toronto: University of Toronto Press.

Karwacki, Judy MR. 1994. "The Two Passions of Pierre Elliott Trudeau: Language and Rights—the Court Challenges Program, 1978–1994." M.A. Thesis, University of Saskatchewan.

Keene, Judith. 1992. *Human Rights In Ontario*. Toronto: Carswell.

Kellogg, Charles Flint. 1967. *NAACP: A History of the National Association for the Advancement of Colored People*. Baltimore: Johns Hopkins Press.

Kennedy, Charles. 1985. "Policies of Redistributional Preference in Pakistan." In *Ethnic Preference and Public Policy in Developing States*, ed. Neil Nevitte and Charles Kennedy. Boulder: Lynne Rienner Publishers.

Kluger, Richard. 1976. *Simple Justice.* New York: Vintage Books.

Knight, Jack, and Lee Epstein. 1996. "On the Struggle for Judicial Supremacy." *Law & Society Review* 30: 87–120.

Knopff, Rainer, and F. L. Morton. 1992. *Charter Politics.* Toronto: Nelson.

Knopff. Rainer. 1989. *Human Rights and Social Technology: The New War on Discrimination.* Ottawa: Carleton University Press.

————, and F. L. Morton. 1985. "Nation-Building and the Canadian Charter of Rights." In *Constitutionalism, Citizenship, and Society in Canada,* ed. Alan Cairns and Cynthia Williams. Toronto: University of Toronto Press.

Koch, John. 1990. "Making Room: New Directions in Third Party Intervention," *University of Toronto Faculty of Law Review* 48: 151–167.

Krislov, Samuel. 1963. "The *Amicus Curiae* Brief: From Friendship to Advocacy," *Yale Law Journal* 72: 694–721.

Lavine, Sharon. 1992. "Advocating Values: Public Interest Intervention in Charter Litigation," *National Journal of Constitutional Law* 2: 27–62.

LEAF. 1986. *Interventions at the Supreme Court of Canada.* Toronto: Women's Legal Education and Action Fund, June.

Levy, Alan. 1972. "The Amicus Curiae (An Offer of Assistance to the Court)," *Chitty's Law Journal* 20: 94–103 and 135–140.

Luce, Duncan R., and Howard Raiffa. 1957. *Games and Decisions.* New York: John Wiley and Sons.

Lustick, Ian. 1979. "Stability in Deeply Divided Societies: Consociationalism versus Control," *World Politics* 31: 325–344.

Lusztig, Michael. 1994. "Constitutional Paralysis: Why Canadian Constitutional Initiatives are Doomed to Fail," *Canadian Journal of Political Science* 27: 747–771.

Mallory, J. R. 1954. *Social Credit and the Federal Power in Canada.* University of Toronto Press.

————. 1944. "The Courts and the Sovereignty of the Canadian Parliament," *Canadian Journal of Economics and Political Science* 10: 165–178.

Mandel, Michael. 1989. *The Charter of Rights and the Legalization of Politics in Canada.* Toronto: Wall and Thompson.

Manfredi, Christopher P. 1993a. *Judicial Power and the Charter: Canada and the Paradox of Liberal Constitutionalism.* Toronto: McClelland and Stewart.

————. 1993b. "Constitutional Rights and Interest Advocacy: Litigating Educational Reform in Canada and the United States." In *Equity and Community: The Charter Interest Advocacy and Representation,* ed. F. Leslie Seidle. Montreal: Institute for Research on Public Policy.

————. 1992. "Litigation and Institutional Design: MicroConstitutional Politics and the Canadian Charter of Rights and Freedoms." Unpublished manuscript.

————. 1991. "*Re Lavigne and Ontario Public Service Employees Union*: Public Administration and Remedial Decree Litigation under the Charter of Rights and Freedoms," *Canadian Public Administration* 34: 395–416.

————. 1990. "The Use of United States Decisions by the Supreme Court of Canada under the Charter of Rights and Freedoms," *Canadian Journal of Political Science* 23: 499–518.

————. 1989. "Adjudication, Policy-Making, and the Supreme Court of Canada: Lessons from the Experience of the United States," *Canadian Journal of Political Science* 22: 313–335.

McCalla, W. 1980. "Locus Standi," *Advocate's Quarterly* 2: 335–340.

McCartney, Patrick A. 1990. "An Examination of Federal and Provincial Government Sponsorship of Voluntary Associations in Canada." M.A. Thesis, Queen's University.

McCormick, Peter. 1994. *Canada's Courts.* Toronto: James Lorimer & Company.

————. 1993. "Party Capability Theory and Appellate Success in the Supreme Court of Canada, 1949–1992," *Canadian Journal of Political Science* 26: 523–540.

————, and Ian Greene. 1990. *Judges and Judging.* Toronto: James Lorimer.

McIntosh, Wayne V 1984. "And Now For Something Completely Different: Amicus Curiae Activity in the Federal District Courts." Presented to the Annual Meetings of the Northeastern Political Science Association, Boston.

———, and Paul E. Parker. 1988. "A Macro-Analytic Assessment of Amicus Intervention in the Federal Courts of Appeals." University of Maryland, College Park. Typescript.

McRae, Kenneth D. 1974. "Consociationalism and the Canadian Political System." In *Political Accommodation in Segmented Societies,* ed. Kenneth D. McRae. Ottawa: Carleton University Press.

Milner, Murray. 1994. *Status and Sacredness: A General Theory of Status Relations and an Analysis of Indian Culture.* New York: Oxford University Press.

Monahan, Patrick. 1987. *Politics and the Constitution: The Charter, Federalism, and the Supreme Court of Canada.* Toronto: Carswell.

———, and Marie Finkelstein. 1993. *The Impact of the Charter on the Public Policy Process.* North York, Ont.: York University Centre for Public Law and Public Policy

Morton, F. L. 1994. "Judicial Politics Canadian-Style: The Supreme Court's Contribution to the Constitutional Crisis of 1992." In *Constitutional Predicament: Canada After the Referendum of 1992,* ed. Curtis Cook. Montreal: McGill-Queen's Press.

———. 1993. "The Charter Revolution and the Court Party." In *The Impact of the Charter on the Public Policy Process,* ed. Patrick Monahan and Marie Finkelstein. North York, Ont.: York University Centre for Public Law and Public Policy.

———. 1992. *Morgentaler v Borowski: Abortion, the Charter, and the Court.* Toronto: McClelland and Stewart.

———. 1989. "The Politics of Rights: What Canadians Should Know About the American Bill of Rights," *Windsor Review of Legal and Social Issues* 1: 6196.

———. "The Political Impact of the Canadian Charter of Rights and Freedoms," *Canadian Journal of Political Science* 20: 31–55.

———. 1984. *Law, Politics, and the Judicial Process in Canada.* University of Calgary Press.

———, and Ian Brodie. 1993. "The Use of Extrinsic Evidence in Charter Litigation Before the Supreme Court of Canada," *National Journal of Constitutional Law* 3: 1–35.

———, and Rainer Knopff. 2000. *The Charter Revolution and the Court Party*. Peterborough: Broadview.

———, Peter H. Russell, and Troy Riddell. 1995. "The *Canadian Charter of Rights and Freedoms*: A Descriptive Analysis of the First Decade, 1982–1992," *National Journal of Constitutional Law* 5: 1–60.

———, Peter H. Russell, and Michael Withey. 1992. "The Supreme Court's First One Hundred Charter of Rights Decisions: A Statistical Analysis." Occasional Papers Series, Research Study 6.1. Calgary: Research Unit for Socio-Legal Studies, The University of Calgary.

Muldoon, Paul R. 1989. *The Law of Intervention: Status and Practice*. Aurora, Ont.: Canada Law Book.

Nevitte, Neil, and Charles Kennedy. 1986. "The Analysis of Policies of Ethnic Preference in Developing States." In *Ethnic Preference and Public Policy in Developing States*, ed. Neil Nevitte and Charles Kennedy. Boulder: Lynne Rienner Publishers.

Niskanen, William A. 1971. *Bureaucracy and Representative Government*. Chicago: Aldine-Atherton.

Nordlinger, Eric A. 1981. *On the Autonomy of the Democratic State*. Cambridge, MA: Harvard University Press.

O'Connor, Karen. 1980. *Women's Organizations' Use of the Courts*. Lexington, MA and Toronto: Lexington Books.

———, and Lee Epstein. 1983. "The Rise of Conservative Interest Group Litigation." *Journal of Politics* 45: 479–489.

O'Connor, Karen, and Lee Epstein. 1981–1982. "Amicus Curiae Participation in US Supreme Court Litigation: An Evaluation of Hakma.n's 'Folklore'," *Law & Society Review* 16: 311–320.

Olson, Mancur. 1971 [1965]. *The Logic of Collective Action: Public Goods and the Theory of Groups*. Cambridge, MA: Harvard University Press.

Olson, Susan. 1990. "Interest Group Litigation in Federal District Court: Beyond the Political Disadvantage Theory," *Journal of Politics* 52: 854–882.

Ostrom, Elinor. 1990. *Governing, the Commons: The Evolution of Institutions for Collective Action*. Cambridge: Cambridge University Press.

Pal, Leslie A. 1993. *Interests of State: The Politics of Language, Multiculturalism, and Feminism in Canada.* Montreal/Kingston: McGill-Queen's Press.

Peltason, Jack. 1955. *Federal Court in the Political Process.* New York: Doubleday.

Pepall, John T. 1996. "What's the Evidence? The Use the Supreme Court Makes of Evidence in Charter Cases." In *Rethinking the Constitution: Perspectives on Canadian Constitutional Reform, Interpretation, and Theory,* ed. Anthony A. Peacock. Don Mills, Ont.: Oxford University Press.

Percy, Steven. 1989. *Disability, Civil Rights, and Public Policy: The Politics of Implementation.* Tuscaloosa: University of Alabama Press.

Pinzler, Isabelle Katz, et al. 1982. "Equal Protection Overview." In *Women Working Together, 13th National Conference on Women and the Law 1982 Sourcebook.* Detroit: 13th National Conference on Women and the Law.

Phillips, Susan D. 1991. "Meaning and Structure in Social Movements: Mapping the Network of National Canadian Women's Organizations," *Canadian Journal of Political Science* 24: 755–782.

Price Waterhouse. 1994. *Department of Canadian Heritage: Court Challenges Program Consultation Report. April 29, 1994.* Ottawa: PriceWaterhouse.

Puro, Steven. 1971. "The Role of the Amicus Curiae in the United States Supreme Court: 1920–1966." Ph.D. Dissertation, State University of New York at Buffalo.

Radwanski, George. 1978. *Trudeau.* Toronto: Macmillan.

Razack, Sherene. 1991. *Canadian Feminism and the Law: The Women's Legal Education and Action Fund and the Pursuit of Equality.* Toronto: Second Story Press.

Riker, William H. 1962. *The Theory of Political Coalitions.* New Haven: Yale University Press.

Roach Kent. 1993. "The Role of Litigation and the Charter in Interest Advocacy." In *Equity and Community,* ed. F. Leslie Seidle. Montreal: IRPP.

Romanow, Roy, John Whyte, and Howard Leeson. 1984. *Canada . . . Notwithstanding.* Toronto: Carswell.

Rosenberg, Gerald. 1991. *The Hollow Hope: Can Courts Bring About Social Change?* Chicago: University of Chicago Press.

Russell, Peter H. 1987. *The Judiciary in Canada: The Third Branch of Government.* Toronto: McGraw-Hill Ryerson.

———. 1983. "Bold Statescraft, Questionable Jurisprudence." In *And No One Cheered: Federalism, Democracy, and the Constitution Act,* ed. Keith G. Banting and Richard E. Simeon. Toronto: Methuen.

———. 1982. "The Effect of a Charter of Rights on the Policy Making Role of Canadian Courts," *Canadian Public Administration* 25: 3–33.

Salisbury, Robert. 1969. "An Exchange Theory of Interest Groups," *Midwest Journal of Political Science* 13: 1–32.

Schelling, Thomas C. 1978. *Micromotives and Macrobehaviour.* Toronto: George J. McLeod.

Scheppele, Kim Lane, and Jack Walker. 1991. "The Litigation Strategies of Interest Groups." In *Mobilizing Interest Groups in America: Patrons, Professions, and Social Movements,* by Jack L. Walker, prepared for publication by Joel D. Aberbach, Frank R. Baumgartner, Thomas L. Gais, David C. King, Mark A. Peterson, and Kim Lane Scheppele. Ann Arbor: University of Michigan Press.

Schmeiser, D. A. 1964. *Civil Liberties in Canada.* London: Oxford University Press.

Scriven, David, and Paul Muldoon. "Intervention as Friend of the Court: Rule 13 of the Ontario Rules of Civil Procedure," *Advocates' Quarterly* 6: 448–472.

Shilton, E. 1992. "Charter Litigation and the Policy Processes of Government." *Osgoode Hall Law Journal* 30: 653–660.

Sigurdson, Richard. 1993. "Left- and Right-Wing Charterphobia in Canada: A Critique of the Critics," *International Journal of Canadian Studies* 7–8: 95–115.

Silverstein, Mark. 1994. *Judicious Choices: The New Politics of Supreme Court Confirmations.* New York: W.W. Norton.

Skocpol, Theda. 1992. *Protecting Soldiers and Mothers: The Political Origins of Social Policy in the United States.* Cambridge, MA: Harvard University Press.

———. 1985. "Bringing the State Back." In *Bringing the State Back In*, Peter B. Evans, Dietrich Rueschemeyer, and Theda Skocpol. New York: Cambridge University Press.

Skogstad, Grace. 1980. "The Farm Products Marketing Agencies Act: A Case Study of Agricultural Policy," *Canadian Public Policy* 6: 89–100.

Smith, Lynn. 1994. "Have the Equality Rights Made Any Difference?" In *Protecting Rights and Freedoms: Essays on the Charter's Place in Canada's Political, Legal, and Intellectual Life*, ed. Philip Bryden, Steven Davis, and John Russell. Toronto: University of Toronto Press.

Sohn, Herbert A. 1975. "Human Rights Legislation in Ontario: A Study of Social Action." Ph.D. Dissertation, University of Toronto.

Songer, Donald, and Reginald Sheehan. 1993. "Interest Group Success in the Courts: Amicus Participation in the Supreme Court," *Political Research Quarterly* 46: 339–354.

———. 1992. "Who Wins on Appeal? Upperdogs and Underdogs in the United States Courts of Appeal," *American Journal of Political Science* 36: 235–258.

Sopinka, John. 1988. "Intervention," *The Advocate* 46: 883– 887.

Steel, Freda M., and Marta J. Smith. 1989. "A Comment on the Application by LEAF for Intervenor Status in *Klachefsky v Brown*," *Canadian Family Law Quarterly* 4: 57–72.

Stone, Alec. 1992. *The Birth of Judicial Politics in France.* Oxford University Press.

Swan, Kenneth P. 1987. "Intervention and Amicus Curiae Status in Charter Litigation." In *Charter Litigation*, ed. Robert J. Sharpe. Toronto: Butterworths.

Tokar, J. 1984. "Administrative Law: Locus Standi in Judicial Review Proceedings," *Manitoba Law Journal* 14: 209–243.

Trudeau, Pierre Elliott. 1968. *Federalism and the French Canadians.* Toronto: MacMillan of Canada.

Truman, David B. 1951. *The Governmental Process: Political Interests and Public Opinion.* New York: Alfred A. Knopf

Tsebelis, George. 1995. "Decision Making in Political Systems: Veto Players in Presidentialism, Parliamentarism, Multicameralism, and Multipartyism," *British Journal of Political Science* 25: 289–325.

———. 1990. *Nested Games: Rational Choice in Comparative Politics.* Berkeley: University of California Press.

Tushnet, Mark V. 1987. *The NAACP's Legal Strategy Against Segregated Education, 1925–1950.* Chapel Hill: University of North Carolina Press.

Vose, Clement. 1959. *Caucasians Only: The Supreme Court, the N.A.A.C.P., and the Restrictive Covenant Cases.* Berkeley: University of California Press.

———. 1958. "Litigation as a Form of Pressure Group Activity," *Annals* 319: 20–31.

———. 1955. "NAACP Strategy in the Covenant Cases," *Western Reserve Law Review* 6: 101–145.

Walker, Jack L. 1983. "The Origins and Maintenance of Interest Groups in America," *American Political Science Review* 77: 390–405.

Wasby, Stephen L. 1995. *Race Relations Litigation in an Age of Complexity.* Charlottesville: University Press of Virginia.

———. 1984. "How Planned is 'Planned Litigation'?" *American Bar Foundation Research Journal* 83: 83–138.

Weiler, Paul. 1974. *In the Last Resort: A Critical Study of the Supreme Court of Canada.* Toronto: Methuen.

———. 1968. "Two Models of Judicial Decision Making," *Canadian Bar Review* 46: 406–471.

Weiner, Gerry. 1992. *Letter to Dr. Bruce Halliday, M.P. Dated December 11, 1992.* Ottawa: Minister of Multiculturalism and Citizenship.

Welch, Jillian. 1985. "No Room at the Top: Interest Group Interveners and *Charter* Litigation in the Supreme Court of Canada," *University of Toronto Faculty of Law Review* 43: 204–231.

West, James V. 1979. "Public Interest Groups and the Judicial Process in Canada: The Need for a More Realistic Jurisprudence." Occasional Paper No. 5, Department of Political Science, Carleton University.

Wheeler, Stanton, Bliss Cartwright, Robert A. Kagan, and Lawrence M. Friedman. 1987. "Do the 'Haves' Come out Ahead? Winning and Losing in State Supreme Courts, 1870–1970," *Law & Society Review* 21: 403–446.

Williams, Cynthia. 1985. "The Changing Nature of Citizen Rights." In *Constitutionalism, State, and Society in Canada*, ed. Alan Cairns and Cynthia Williams. Toronto: University of Toronto Press.

Wilson, Bertha. 1988. "The Making of a Constitution: Approaches to Judicial Interpretation," *Public Law:* 370–384.

———. 1986. "Decision–Making in the Supreme Court," *University of Toronto Law Journal* 36: 227–248.

Wiseman, Nelson. 1992. "The Questionable Relevance of the Constitution in Advancing Minority Cultural Rights in Manitoba," *Canadian Journal of Political Science* 25: 697–721.

# INDEX